Something Happens Here

Something Happens Here

*Reclaiming the Distinctiveness of Wesley's
Communion Spirituality in Times of Divisiveness*

Stephen P. West

Foreword by Don E. Saliers

WIPF & STOCK · Eugene, Oregon

SOMETHING HAPPENS HERE
Reclaiming the Distinctiveness of Wesley's Communion Spirituality in Times of Divisiveness

Copyright © 2022 Stephen Pierce West. All rights reserved. Except for brief quotations in critical publications or reviews, no part of this book may be reproduced in any manner without prior written permission from the publisher. Write: Permissions, Wipf and Stock Publishers, 199 W. 8th Ave., Suite 3, Eugene, OR 97401.

Wipf & Stock
An Imprint of Wipf and Stock Publishers
199 W. 8th Ave., Suite 3
Eugene, OR 97401

www.wipfandstock.com

PAPERBACK ISBN: 978-1-6667-3880-3
HARDCOVER ISBN: 978-1-6667-9992-7
EBOOK ISBN: 978-1-6667-9993-4

08/05/22

Scripture quotations are from New Revised Standard Version Bible: Anglicized Edition, copyright © 1989, 1995 National Council of the Churches of Christ in the United States of America. Used by permission. All rights reserved worldwide.

All quotes of Wesley hymns are retained in the original form from the first edition of *Hymns on the Lord's Supper with a Preface Concerning the Christian Sacrament and Sacrifice, Extracted from Doctor Brevint*, 1745. Unusual spelling, capitalization, and italicizing of words for emphasis will be unaltered. However, the archaic long *s* (*f*) has been changed to *s* to facilitate ease of reading.

"Who better than pastor, scholar, musician Steve West to minister to us in the present moment, calling us Wesleyans to the core of our dynamic sacramental piety? Amid the threatened sad separations and acrimonious debate in our church, Steve gives an irenic, passionate, celebratory, deeply Christian witness that could lead us, by God's grace, into a more hopeful future."

—WILL WILLIMON, retired United Methodist bishop

"In a time when it's important to come back to the table instead of just going our separate ways, Steve invites us into real community and a radical life. . . . Steve shares his imagination with us in a way that gives us not only deeper appreciation for hymnology but practical application for all it means to be a time traveler with him."

—GLANDION W. CARNEY, Anglican priest, retired

"West takes us on a journey behind John Wesley's understanding of Communion to earlier sources and then through John's writings and his brother Charles's hymns. However, West is not really focusing on the sacramental theology—he is focusing *through* it. His real concern is how a Wesleyan understanding of the table can inform the faithfulness of the church in the midst of intense division. A timely book."

—O. WESLEY ALLEN, JR., Southern Methodist University

"In clear prose, West's study delivers historical, theological, and pastoral explanations of the eucharistic celebration's immanent potential for forming the assembled members in Christlike charity and service revealed through word and sacrament."

—BRUCE T. MORRILL, SJ, Vanderbilt University

"Feast on this book, and it will help you feast on God's grace! West has taken the riches of the Wesleys' theology of Holy Communion and made them available for the church today in a way that's both historically rigorous and remarkably relevant. He has shown that reconnecting with the breadth, depth, and beauty of this holy meal is the best path toward a hopeful future for the church."

—**L. ROGER OWENS**, Pittsburgh Theological Seminary

"West immerses us in the Wesleyan theology and practice of Holy Communion, especially at this moment fraught with schism. West invites a reconsideration of Wesley's emphases on the real presence, remembrance as 'experiencing anew,' and the sacramental work of the Holy Spirit. In fact, the epiclesis embodies the full expression of Wesleyan eucharistic spirituality. *Something Happens Here* is a compelling and essential read for a people in need of hope and a reformed identity."

—**RICHARD L. ESLINGER**, United Theological Seminary, emeritus

"West's book is an interesting, must-read intersection of pastoral and scholarly perspectives that can aid United Methodist and other clergy and laity in reclaiming the sacrament of Holy Communion. Following John and Charles Wesley, . . . West suggests to the divisive forces in the church—indeed, to all—to first come to the table of the Lord. There alone is guidance for the individual's and the church's direction now and in the future."

—**S T KIMBROUGH, JR.**, Duke Divinity School

*Dedicated to the memory of
Richmond Pierce West,
who inspired me to do this*

This is what God's kingdom is like:
a bunch of outcasts and oddballs gathered at a table,
not because they are rich or worthy or good,
but because they are hungry,
because they said yes.
And there's always room for more.

—RACHEL HELD EVANS

Contents

Foreword by Don E. Saliers | ix
About This Book | xiii
Acknowledgements | xv
Prelude | xvii

1. Communion as a Prism | 1
2. The Mystery of Presence | 9
3. Experiencing Anew | 26
4. Becoming All Flame | 41
5. Foretaste of Heaven | 63
6. Grand Channel of Grace | 79
7. Becoming the Body | 92
8. Reconnecting | 107

Postlude | 129
About the Author | 141
Bibliography | 143

Foreword

AT THE HEART OF Wesleyan theology is a way of life grounded in the life-giving word and sacrament of the table. In these pages, my friend Steve West opens a treasure of insights into John Wesley's teaching and Charles Wesley's hymns. There is a complex history behind the development of a Wesleyan sacramental theology. In this book, we are introduced to that history made lively by the author's own pastoral experience. There is research and learning here combined with a faithful commitment to a Wesleyan way of life.

You will discover here, as I have, a way of receiving John Wesley's admonition to unite what is too often divided: "knowledge and vital piety."[1] The author knows that reason and faith belong fully together. Each chapter focuses on a distinctive historical aspect of a full Wesleyan sacramental theology. At every point, the reader is guided by stories from actual church life in the author's pastoral experience. In sum, this book provides an authentic pastoral/theological approach to some of the most central ideas essential to understanding a distinctive Wesleyan theological form of reasoning. In the process, we are shown both the shaping of Wesley's thought and the spiritual power of his legacy to the churches.

Many of us are aware of the current struggles in the Methodist church traditions for integrity and self-understanding. In a time of confusion and lack of clarity, West calls us to examine the

---

1. Charles Wesley, "Come, Father, Son, and Holy Ghost," in The Methodist Church, *Methodist Hymnal*, 344.

Foreword

essentials: What is the meaning of Christ's sacramental presence? What is it to be a community of love and justice grounded in a redemptive meal of grace? What is it to begin to practice a way of life that flows from the words and actions of Christ at the table?

The book opens with the image of a prism. Just as light strikes a prism to generate a wide and comprehensive spectrum of colors, so Scripture—especially in the Gospels and Paul's writings on the Eucharist—open our eyes to the depth of sacramental life in Christ. This can serve as a basic image for reading the whole book. As we move through each chapter, focusing upon various strands of influence on Wesley's development, it is like turning a diamond in the light. The breadth of his theology begins to emerge. While each contributing influence is distinctive, together they help us see both the depth and breadth of Wesley's more mature views. One way to read the book, then, is to regard each chapter as a turning of a prism, attending to how each influence contributes to the whole illuminating pattern of thought and practice.

Both of the Wesleys insist on biblical foundations, but always in the light of living tradition. So, we learn that the English Nonjurors had an especially strong role in shaping the roots of early Methodist thought in Great Britain. There we see a skillful negotiation of more conservative social/political views with an accent on communitarian concerns in the formation of a theology of the church engaged in society. Alongside this, we come to see that the question of divine presence is profoundly linked for the Wesleys with embodiment of grace in piety and social conscience.

Some readers will be especially interested in Wesley's reading and understanding of early Christian monastic writers such as Macarius. There we see how clearly Wesleyan thought avoids excessive preoccupation with cognitive understanding. There is an indebtedness to this patristic and even mystical (in the best sense) dimension of John Wesley's theology of divine presence in the world. This illuminates the nondogmatic dimensions of his emerging sacramental theology.

One cannot help thinking of John's attraction to German pietist hymns of, say, Paul Gerhard and others. While not as much

Foreword

attention is given to Charles Wesley's hymns here, this aspect of the book helps me see the richness of how Methodists came to "sing" our sacramental theology. This could be called the "lyrical" prism of doctrine in practice.

Reading these pages, I am reminded that we know so little about the richness of our own theological tradition with respect to the Eucharist. I invite you to receive this study (and witness) as a gift. As a theologian of worship and spirituality, my sincere desire is that we raise up a new generation of pastoral teachers like the author of this welcome volume.

Good theology contributes to strong and mature practice. In times like ours, this is a welcome gift. Whatever the deficiencies in the Wesleys' eighteenth-century views, recent sacramental thought has deepened the essentials we discover in these pages.

Don E. Saliers
theologian in residence
Candler School of Theology, Emory University

About This Book

THE UNITED METHODIST CHURCH is at a crossroads in history. In seasons of change and uncertainty, nothing could be more important than reclaiming our sacramental distinctiveness in these times of great divisiveness. There is something about life at the table that both *reflects* and *informs* our journey as we move forward.

Comprehensive yet coherent, this book takes a fresh look at John Wesley's core teachings on the Lord's Supper. It is not just for clergy. It is for all who hunger and thirst for God. Without posturing on the politics of our day, the author brings Wesley's Communion theology to light and lets each unique feature serve as a lens to help navigate troubled waters into the future. He explores the historical background of each unique characteristic of Wesley's teaching on the Eucharist, uncovers evidence of them in the writings of John and Charles Wesley, and applies them to the struggles of present-day United Methodism. He concludes with signs of new life emerging in our divisive times, as people come back to the table to move forward into the future.

Readers will grapple with the idea that Communion is not just a personal experience with Jesus but a feast that has huge implications for our life together. They will be given language to define themselves against sacramental theology colored by other denominations in their communities. Along the way, they will discover tools to thoughtfully sort through difficult conversations about divisive matters rather than settling into the either-or and

xiii

About This Book

"us against them" mentalities that pervade national conversations about culture wars.

This book does not settle for the task of bringing the liturgy to life. It leads us to discover the shape of the life of the church in front of us. In the end, the author points to some of the ways coming back to the table will be what propels us forward in our struggle for new beginnings.

Acknowledgements

I AM FILLED WITH gratitude for a kaleidoscope of people who made this possible. I would like to thank Don Saliers and Bruce Morrill for nudging me to share my work in the form of a book. I wish to thank the excellent faculty and staff of Sewanee: The University of the South for providing me with the academic challenge and insightful direction to do this. I am appreciative of the many wisdom teachers, staff, and friends of the Upper Room and the Academy for Spiritual Formation for grounding my passion for God in the depths of Christian spirituality and history. I would like to acknowledge countless souls, such as Nina Reeves and Kelley Neal, for nurturing me spiritually at Camp Sumatanga and rooting my spiritual development in Christ's table. I thank the sisters of Sacred Heart Monastery for providing gracious hospitality over the years and introducing me to the world of spiritual formation studies. I'm incredibly grateful for Lesley Cooper, Brent Waltrip, and Lucy Wray, who have been long-term companions in my covenant group.

Most of all, I want to thank the people of the local churches I have served for showing me what it means to love with the love of Christ in the beautiful messiness of Christian community. Specifically, I thank the people of Arab First United Methodist Church for allowing me some time and financial support to do my doctoral work while serving there joyfully. Finally, I would like to thank my life companion, Sandy O'Quinn West, my father, Pete West, and

Acknowledgements

my dear children and other relatives for their love and emotional support during this journey.

Prelude

IF THERE IS SUCH a thing as a mind-blowing story about Holy Communion, I have one. A dear pastor friend named John Rutland had been close to my family since long before I was born. He was one of the old-time Methodist preachers of the North Alabama Conference, always wearing a white shirt, a blazer or sport coat, a super-wide tie, and an even wider love for Jesus. He had a spring in his step and a twinkle in his eye, and to me, this short, stocky man was always larger than life.

He and my dad had been colleagues in ministry, and John loved to tell of a time he gave me a quarter when I was a child and he was my father's district superintendent. Apparently, I got up in his lap and said, "Brother Rutland, when you go to that place . . ."

He said, "You mean annual conference?"

"Yes, and you see that man . . ."

He responded, "You mean the bishop?"

"Yes, will you tell him to send my daddy to Disney World?"

John had told me plenty of stories, though his Communion story brought them all together for me. My wife and I had become associate pastors at the same church he served in his retirement, and he told me numerous tales from his years of preaching in the middle of Birmingham's civil rights history and his uncanny tendency to step into it. He once took me to the pulpit area of the old Woodlawn United Methodist Church and pointed to a seating

Prelude

section on the far right, near the exit. "That's where Bull Conner used to sit . . . when he was sitting, that is."

I knew, of course, of the infamous commissioner in Birmingham that oversaw the police and fire departments, enforcing segregation and becoming a national symbol of police brutality with police dogs and fire hoses. Conner had been a member of that church during the civil rights era when Rutland pastored there. "Sometimes, when I would preach that Jesus loved all people, regardless of the color of their skin, he would stand up, huff, and storm out."

Standing by the pulpit that day, he told me the colorful story of the time he walked up to Conner and his deputies standing on the front steps of the church with their arms crossed. After he asked what they were doing, Conner said, "We're making sure only the appropriate people come to church today."

John got up in his face with a pointed finger and said, "Let me tell you something, Mr. Conner. I am the pastor of this church, and I've been appointed by the bishop to serve this church. I will decide who can come in for worship. And if you get in my way, I'll call your own police department and have you removed." He then walked away, his legs feeling like limp noodles.

As he rounded the corner, he heard Conner whisper to his deputies, "Let's go, boys. He'll do it."

John Rutland must be one of the few people that Bull Conner backed down from.

On another occasion, John told me of a letter he had once gotten from the well-known Alabama governor George Wallace. He had been with a group of preachers who had met with Wallace a few weeks prior to his first inauguration, a meeting where he had made all sorts of promises to these pastors, who were in favor of integrating schools. Then at the inauguration, Wallace made the infamous speech with the words "Segregation now . . . segregation tomorrow . . . segregation forever!"[1]

John was perplexed and wrote Wallace a letter asking how he could possibly change his tune so dramatically in such a short

---

1. Wallace, *Inaugural Address*, 5.

Prelude

period of time. Wallace wrote back to him, saying, "I've been out-segged [referring to segregation], and I'm not going to be out-segged again . . . you fancy-pants preachers had better watch your backs in Alabama."

You can imagine how I felt when Rutland walked into my office one day with a story that blew my mind and said, "I wish you'd been here yesterday."

I had been visiting the hospitals, and boy was I sorry.

"I dropped by to see if you wanted to go with me to serve Communion to George Wallace." He then told me one of the most compelling stories about Holy Communion I have ever heard.

Our bishop, Lloyd Knox, had called John Rutland to ask if he had a portable Communion set. Governor Wallace, still a Methodist, had called Bishop Knox from his deathbed and asked if he would come serve him Communion. The bishop had been busy preparing to move away from the annual conference at the end of his term, so his Communion set was already packed. "John, I want you to go with me to serve Communion."

"Bishop, I'd be glad to loan you my Communion set, but I really don't think you want me to go visit George Wallace with you." As John put it, the bishop could be very persuasive, as bishops can be. He went after all, hoping that Wallace wouldn't recognize him, since it had been so many years.

But as soon as he walked into the room, Wallace looked at him and said in a booming voice, "John Rutland!"

He sheepishly walked in. The bishop gathered them around the hospital bed and asked why he wanted to receive Communion. Wallace said, "I asked you to come today because for so many years, I was wrong. I was wrong about a lot of things." He shared that he needed to make his peace with God.

Bishop Knox went and got the nurse out of the hallway, and she happened to be African American. They all shared the holy meal together.

John finished his story with words I will never forget: "Here we were—Bishop Knox, George Wallace, a Black nurse, and the 'fancy-pants preacher' sharing Communion together. Now that's the kingdom of God!"

It certainly is.

In Methodist tradition, Communion is a sacrament, an outward and visible sign of an inward and spiritual grace. The fullness of the mystery of Communion can never be reduced to obediently performing a ritual, or an object lesson to remind us of the meaning of the cross, or a transaction where we dutifully exchange confession for forgiveness. Deep in our Methodist bones, we know that there is more to Holy Communion. Something happens here, and John Rutland taught me how to see it.

Communion has a way of shedding light on both who we really are and who we are called to be. It is an honest meal. We come to the table being real with God through confession, and Christ comes to us in real ways though his presence, hospitality, and grace. The Lord's Supper binds us together in ways beyond words, for it is a sacred act of both receiving the grace of God and being the body of Christ with one another.

John Rutland's story stuck with me during the rest of my life and ministry because it is not just a tale about race relations. It was a crystallized moment in time that sheds light on the power of this holy meal. We taste and see the goodness of the Lord. We get an honest look at who we are, experience how incredibly beloved by God we are, and get a glimpse of life in the kingdom while we are at it. No, there is nothing magical about the Communion table. A better word for it would be "mystical."

While the civil rights movement as we knew it is in the past (though racism continues to rear its ugly head), the church in North America is at another crossroads with an array of complex questions about human sexuality. No two periods in history are completely alike, of course. But two things will always remain the same: the fundamental call to love as Christ loves and the mysterious intersection of Holy Communion with what it means to be Christian community. In times of deep disunity, it is not so much that Communion can serve as a corrective for us. It is better to say that Communion can become *connective* for us. We need to reconnect

Prelude

with God and each other in new and fresh ways, especially in these difficult times when culture wars threaten to pull us apart.

For those of us who find our home in the United Methodist Church, nothing is more important than reclaiming our sacramental distinctiveness in these times of great divisiveness. The purpose of this book is to take a careful look at John Wesley's core teachings on the Lord's Supper. I believe that our unique Communion spirituality must be the prism through which we behold the colors of life and love together. We long to see clearly because, simply put, our life at the table is at stake.

It is my hope that this book will bring Wesley's Communion theology to light for such a time as this. His teaching on Holy Communion had some unique features. I will do my best to illuminate each one in a way that serves as a lens to help navigate troubled waters into the future. I invite you on a journey with me into the heart of the Lord's Supper, which Wesley called the "grand channel of grace."[2]

As we observe each special trait of his teaching on the sacrament, we will first explore an influential person or group in history that shaped it. This brings an incredible level of depth to our reading of Wesley, and it gives us context. Next, we will uncover evidence of each unique feature in the writings of John and Charles Wesley themselves, whether it is in hymn texts, sermons, or Scripture notes. Finally, we will begin to apply each one to the struggles of present-day United Methodism. We will then see how these remarkable characteristics of Wesleyan Communion theology are all wrapped together in Wesley's concept of the sacrament as a "means of grace" and are plain to see in our United Methodist Communion liturgy. We will close our journey by beginning to ask how reconnecting with the special nature of our life at the table will see us into the future.

It is my deepest longing that this book will do more than bring our Communion liturgy to life—that it will help us discover the life of the church in front of us. I invite you to a path of discovering ways that coming back to the table will be what propels us forward

---

2. Outler and Heitzenrater, *John Wesley's Sermons*, 232.

Prelude

in our struggle for new beginnings. After all, Jesus himself is the one that connected this most sacred meal with the emergence of the kingdom of God, saying, "I tell you, I will never again drink of this fruit of the vine until that day when I drink it new with you in my Father's kingdom."[3] This meal has always been broken and shared while looking forward. This book is both a product of uncertain times when we need to reconnect with our deepest roots and the result of a lifelong hunger that keeps me coming back to the table of grace. I hope that as the reader, you will find yourself saying what John Rutland dared to say: "Now that's the kingdom of God!"

3. Matt 26:29.

1

Communion as a Prism

I KEEP A SMALL prism in a box on a shelf, near my books on the sacraments and Communion. I've been fascinated by prisms since I first encountered them in elementary school, those little transparent, triangle-shaped rods with polished surfaces that refract light. When you turn them a certain way, you can see colors that you could not see before, though we know the colors come from the one true light. They are so radiant and beautiful.

In my reflections over the years, the prism has become my beloved metaphor for understanding the apostle Paul's way of teaching about Holy Communion. Like no other writer in the New Testament, Paul wants us to see the vibrant colors of our life and love together through a certain lens. I propose that he holds up Communion as a prism for all to see, and for all time. My observation of what happens in the long stretch between 1 Cor 11 through 1 Cor 15 is that he held Communion up to the light for a shimmering view. Then he turned it, and turned it repeatedly, to see things going on in the community in a new way.

Most of us have probably read these chapters as if they were stand-alone works almost independent from one another. This is a by-product of the Western church's tendency to teach Bible verses as lonely snippets and chapters, as if they were self-contained silos, when we should be searching for Scripture's overarching truths. These chapters are most definitely not freestanding; they are intentionally threaded together by Paul. Let me show you what I mean.

A quick look at the beginning of 1 Corinthians shows there were problems in the early church of Corinth. Paul pulls no punches, for he had heard they were in divisive times:

> Now I appeal to you, brothers and sisters, by the name of our Lord Jesus Christ, that all of you should be in agreement and that there should be no divisions among you, but that you should be united in the same mind and the same purpose.[1]

Some of these divisions must have felt rather personal, since they connected with his own ministry there in the past:

> For it has been reported to me by Chloe's people that there are quarrels among you, my brothers and sisters. What I mean is that each of you says, "I belong to Paul," or "I belong to Apollos," or "I belong to Cephas," or "I belong to Christ." Has Christ been divided? Was Paul crucified for you? Or were you baptized in the name of Paul?[2]

I don't know who "Chloe's people" were, but I do know churches and how we have a natural propensity to have our "people." That's nothing new. Paul continues with some memories of who he had personally baptized there and remarks that he was glad there weren't very many. That way, nobody could say they were baptized in *his* name. In Paul's time, like too many times since, the divisions of the community found a focal point in what leader they identified with. Again, that's nothing new.

When you read chapters 11–15 as one body of thought, as I am suggesting, this conflict in the community is the backdrop on which he shines the metaphorical Communion prism: "Now in the following instructions I do not commend you, because when you come together it is not for the better but for the worse."[3] I suppose nothing could be harsher than saying to a church—named from

---

1. 1 Cor 1:10.
2. 1 Cor 1:11–13.
3. 1 Cor 11:17.

Communion as a Prism

the word *ecclesia* in New Testament Greek, which literally means "gathering"—that when you get together, you are worse off than when you started. "For, to begin with, when you come together as a church, I hear that there are divisions among you; and to some extent I believe it."[4] Paul says that a good look at these factions will make it clear who is genuine, and he holds up the Communion lens to show them a glimpse of what he has been saying: "When you come together, it is not really to eat the Lord's supper. For when the time comes to eat, each of you goes ahead with your own supper, and one goes hungry and another becomes drunk."[5] I have often mused that we might not want to tell friends from some of the other North American denominations how clear it is that Jesus, the disciples, and the early church freely imbibed. Paul does wonder why they don't just do that at home if they are going to get drunk. It might be hard to wrap our minds around Paul here until we remember that in the early church, the Communion ritual and the fellowship supper were not two separate experiences, as they tend to be in modern church life. This was highly sacramental fellowship. It was an enjoyable meal with a Communion component and a generally sacred character. It represented the fullness of Christian sharing, and they did it each and every Sunday (early Christians began gathering on Sundays, the day of the resurrection, rather than on the Sabbath sometime in the first century).

When Paul held up the prism and showed them what they were doing at the weekly community meal and Communion table, he was showing them the divisions that were lying beneath the surface. Communion was the *real* deal because it showed them what was *really* there: divisions which were disregarded and might even have gone unnoticed. "Or do you show contempt for the church of God and humiliate those who have nothing?"[6]

Then he turns the hand to show us something else. What follows is the most extensive reflection on the institution of the Lord's Supper in all of Scripture:

4. 1 Cor 11:18.
5. 1 Cor 11:20–21.
6. 1 Cor 11:22b.

Something Happens Here

> For I received from the Lord what I also handed on to you, that the Lord Jesus on the night when he was betrayed took a loaf of bread, and when he had given thanks, he broke it and said, "This is my body that is for you. Do this in remembrance of me."[7]

In the same way, he shares that Jesus took the cup and spoke of the new covenant in Christ's blood. What follows (and what makes Paul's version stand apart from the narratives in the Gospels) is some theological reflection, with a slight twist of the hand holding the Communion lens:

> Whoever, therefore, eats the bread or drinks the cup of the Lord in an unworthy manner will be answerable for the body and blood of the Lord. Examine yourselves, and only then eat of the bread and drink the cup. For all who eat and drink without discerning the body, eat and drink judgment against themselves.[8]

Drop the mic. Paul even assumes this is why so many of them have taken ill. I suppose spiritual sickness takes its toll on the body.

Let's stop here and discuss something that's extremely important, because this scripture has often been misused. It could be read through the eyes of a Pharisee, with the tendency to make Communion into another form of "works righteousness." If you do Communion in an unworthy manner, you drink judgment on yourselves, so you'd better "get your heart right before God" (a phrase that rubs against my spiritual grain). Paul's "unworthy manner" has nothing to do with purity of heart, or pristine personal morality, or whether you are acting seriously as opposed to being casual (this is, after all, a fellowship dinner Paul was looking at). It's not just about good table manners, but it has everything to do with regard for others. The context of this statement, like the context of the entire book, is that people weren't loving each other with the love of God.

---

7. 1 Cor 11:23–24.
8. 1 Cor 11:27–29.

Communion as a Prism

So then, my brothers and sisters, when you come together to eat, wait for one another. If you are hungry, eat at home, so that when you come together, it will not be for your condemnation.[9]

The "unworthy manner" he pointed out was not a private matter of the heart but entirely about what Wesley called "social holiness."[10]

After this chapter, Paul turns the glass to show us more vivid color. For most of my life, I thought this was a change of subject leading into a stand-alone chapter, but it is not. "Now concerning spiritual gifts, brothers and sisters, I do not want you to be uninformed."[11] Believing there are varieties of gifts but the same Spirit who activates them in everyone, he lays out Paul's favorite and often-repeated image of what it means to be the body of Christ, the metaphor of the human body: "For just as the body is one and has many members, and all the members of the body, though many, are one body, so it is with Christ."[12] He goes into a lengthy discussion about how one part of the body can't say to another, "I don't need you." We are the body of Christ, and each one of us is one of the body parts. This is a practical and easily understandable biblical metaphor for who we are as the church. What I have begun to see is that he's still holding up a prism. He's still talking about the disregard for others he saw in their poor Communion practices, and he's laying out an alternative. We are called to see each other differently than the classism he saw evident at the holy meal. My claim that there is an overarching theme in these chapters is confirmed as he concludes chapter 12 with these words: "And I will show you a still more excellent way."[13]

This phrase was Paul's conspicuous way of turning the lens once again to show us a little more color, to show us something even better than the word picture he had just spent a chapter on.

9. 1 Cor 11:33–34.
10. Wesley and Wesley, *Sacred Poems*, viii.
11. 1 Cor 12:1.
12. 1 Cor 12:12.
13. 1 Cor 12:31b.

Something Happens Here

He goes into what is called the "love chapter" in common church-speak. "If I speak in the tongues of mortals and of angels, but do not have love, I am a noisy gong or a clanging cymbal."[14] He says if he has prophetic powers, attains infinite knowledge, or gives away everything but does not have love, he's nothing. He's just finished a discussion on spiritual gifts in the chapter before, but without love, speaking in tongues is nothing more than percussion noise. Even the beauty of the diversity of gifts in the body of Christ means nothing without love.

I've heard 1 Cor 13 read at too many weddings to possibly count, but it has occurred to me that it *wasn't* written for weddings. It was written to give the people of Corinth better perspective on church conflict. It was written because Christianity is more than refraining from hogging all the food and the wine (though that's a viable step toward community for sure). Christianity is even more than the additional insight of seeing others positively as beloved gifts of God. It's the "more excellent way," a way of patience and kindness that "bears all things" and "believes all things," that "hopes all things" and "endures all things."[15] Anything less is like seeing through a dark pane of glass. "And now faith, hope, and love abide, these three; and the greatest of these is love."[16]

It might seem fitting to stop there, at the pinnacle of his theological expression. But Paul doesn't do that. Instead, he turns the prism once again to shed some more light on practical matters related to how they regard each other. Apparently, some of the people of Corinth—perhaps the very folks who ate and drank with such abandon—thought rather highly of their gift of speaking in tongues. He turns the glass as he begins the chapter with "Pursue love and strive for the spiritual gifts, and especially that you may prophesy."[17] The rest of chapter 14 is an argument that this gift is greater than the fantastic gift of tongues because it builds up the church, while speaking in tongues just builds up yourself.

14. 1 Cor 13:1.
15. 1 Cor 12:31, 13:7.
16. 1 Cor 13:13.
17. 1 Cor 14:1.

Communion as a Prism

It's a beautiful gift, but perhaps in Paul's time, like ours, the gift of tongues was seen as somehow head and shoulders above the rest, reflecting a deep spiritual arrogance. But it is only useful if it builds other people up. All of worship, he says, and every gift we offer is for the purpose of building up the body of Christ.

After all this, chapter 15 may seem like a sudden shift into a teaching on the basics of the gospel and the resurrection of the dead, but notice the opening words, which turn the figurative prism once again: "Now I should remind you, brothers and sisters, of the good news that I proclaimed to you, which you in turn received, in which also you stand."[18] He then summarizes the gospel narrative, concluding with the risen Christ's mystical appearance to him personally on the road to Damascus. Finally, he provides a brief treatise on the resurrection of the dead. Ultimately, he is turning the Communion prism to reveal the light of the kingdom of heaven.

After this, Paul concludes 1 Corinthians with a final chapter on practical matters like taking collections for missions and planning his travel.[19] But in these five chapters we have explored, Paul has moved from observing what is happening at the table and the divisiveness and lack of regard it reveals to an elaborate metaphor on being the body of Christ with different but vitally important parts, to a poetic theology on love as an even more excellent way, to instructions about using your gifts in a way that builds other people up, to taking a glimpse toward the afterlife to put it all in perspective. All this is one body of thought, and Communion was the prism through which he saw all this and communicated the colors of our life and love together.

I invite you to do with me what Paul did. I invite you to lift up Holy Communion as the lens by which we see the vibrant colors of what love must mean for us. It can be a luminous task in this liminal space we find ourselves in. Just as Paul held the Lord's Supper up to the light and let his theology emerge from the colors he began to see, I suggest that John Wesley did the same thing

18. 1 Cor 15:1.
19. 1 Cor 16.

in his time. He did so during difficult times in England and early America when he was lighting a fire that would eventually become the Methodist Episcopal Church, a kindling of the Spirit that was not without criticism and strife—due, in part, to the American Revolution. It is my desire that this book take you on a journey of holding up Communion to the light with Wesley to see its vivid colors as he saw them. Perhaps then we can reclaim this distinctiveness for our times of divisiveness, so that we might discover again how lifting up our life at the table before the light of God will help us to see what we *need* to see.

The following chapters invite you to do just that with Wesley. I'll begin with the most shimmering light he saw, the light of *presence*. For John Wesley, Communion is all about Christ's *real* presence in our Communion gatherings. This is the key to Wesley's Communion theology.

I will then suggest that holding this prism, glowing in the light of the presence of Christ, Wesley begins to turn it to different angles to show us the various colors that emerge from the energy of that presence. First, he shows us the brilliant colors of what Christ called *remembrance* as we experience in a fresh way the sacrifice of Christ in our present gathering around the table. Second, he displays the dazzling colors of *sanctification*, suggesting that Holy Communion is a key to nourishing our personal growth in what he calls "Christian perfection" in love.[20] Third, he exhibits the gleaming colors of building Christian *community* as a foretaste of heaven. I propose that these are distinct arrangements of color in Wesley's theology that reflect the vivid presence of Christ in Holy Communion. This has an uncanny resemblance to the flow of thought in 1 Corinthians! With Wesley's Communion prism in mind, we will then look at how he capsulates this theology in the phrase "means of grace" and uncover clues of this light unfolding in our United Methodist liturgy. We will then conclude with signs of new life emerging in our divisive times as people come back to the table to move forward into the future.

---

20. See Outler and Heitzenrater, *John Wesley's Sermons*, 69–84.

2

The Mystery of Presence

I was reared attending summer camp at a retreat center in the mountains of north Alabama. It is called Sumatanga, a Himalayan word for a place of vision and rest, and it is a heartwarming place. A friend has often remarked that those of us who love this setting tend to "see heaven as a pale reflection of Sumatanga."

There is a tradition that helped me "taste and see" the mystery of Christ's presence in the corporate gathering for the Lord's Supper, and that is the closing Communion and candlelight circle on the last night of summer camp. Communion was the focal point of the final night, usually served "in the round" in a warmly lit setting in the Assembly Hall, with earthy chalices and freshly baked bread. After receiving it, we went out one by one to become part of a great circle in the Chigger Bowl, a grassy field below and across the dirt road. We lit our candles, had closing devotions, and headed off to bed in Benedictine silence. The experience of the night felt as if Christ was really there. And he was. We were often taught that Christ was not in the bread and juice that were somehow changed, but he was present . . . yes, *really* present . . . in our gathering as the body of Christ that night. Christ's presence was sparkling with light.

Something Happens Here

The purpose of this chapter is to get in touch with that mystery. If Communion is a prism, Christ presence floods the main body of the lens, glistening with the fullness of light. First, I would like to identify where this idea of presence originally comes from in Wesleyan spirituality, for it was born out of the influence of the English Nonjurors on John Wesley.

The English Nonjurors

The Nonjurors were a schismatic minority in the Church of England after what is called the Glorious Revolution of 1688 and 1689, a generation before John and Charles Wesley came on the scene. Nonjurors stood together in opposition to the deposing of James II, the last Catholic monarch of England, in favor of "William and Mary," his Anglican daughter Mary Stuart and her Protestant husband, William of Orange.[1] They were called Nonjurors, which means "non-swearers," because as conscientious objectors, they were unwilling to swear allegiance to the new king and queen. They saw this as a violation of their sworn recognition of James and his successors as rightful heirs, for James had recently had a son.

Like any religious movement, it took on its own theological life. Nonjurors became particularly interested in simple Christianity and recovering the ancient liturgies of the church. Let us have a look at the way the Nonjurors began to understand Christ's "real" presence in the gathering itself as one of the deepest mysteries of Communion. The word "sacrament" comes from the Greek *mysterion*, meaning "hidden" or "secret." For these English clergy, Christ was mystically present in "virtue [meaning quality], power, and effect," three words that are repeated numerous times in their writings.[2] Wesley adopted this into his spirituality of life at the table.

---

1. Hefling, "Episcopalians and Nonjurors," 168.

2. The language of "virtue, power, and effect" will be referenced several times. For Nonjurors, the elements do not change in substance but are representations that become the body and blood of Christ in virtue (or quality), having the power and effect of Christ's presence (see "Holy Eucharist, Doctrine of" in Ollard, *English Church History*, 279–82).

The Mystery of Presence

John Wesley was an Anglican priest and missionary both in England and in the Oglethorpe colony of early Georgia history, and his ministry was not done in a vacuum. Wesley's writings were shaped by his missionary experience for sure, but his theological threads come from early eighteenth-century Anglican life. John Wesley was driven by a burning desire to see his mission work in Georgia as a laboratory for trying out simple, early church Christianity. Geordan Hammond puts it succinctly in an article on Wesley's ideal for "primitive" Christianity:

> The ideal of primitive Christianity exerted a profound influence on John Wesley (1703–1791) during the last few years he spent at Oxford before making the bold decision to become a missionary in the recently established colony in Georgia (chartered in 1732). This impulse to restore the purity of the early church was an established tradition within mainstream Anglicanism that was mediated to Wesley through his high church predecessors including his parents, and the nonjurors, Anglicans who declined to take the Oaths of Allegiance and Supremacy to William and Mary.[3]

John Bowmer also says that Wesley "was profoundly influenced by the Nonjurors in their emulation of the pre-Nicene Church."[4] Wesley picked this up from them, and their Communion theology affected his lifelong ministry as well as the sacramental life of the colonial mission in what would become the state of Georgia in the United States.

There are several liturgical practices in Wesley's ministry that are distinctive to the Nonjurors and embedded in the fabric of John Wesley's Communion theology. The Nonjuror emphasis on Christ's presence in "virtue, power, and effect" essentially served as a theological nest for the Wesleyan understanding of Communion.

It might be helpful to share some historical background. As I have said, the Nonjurors opposed removing James II from the throne in favor of William and Mary and were unwilling to swear

---

3. Hammond, "High Church Anglican Influences," 174.
4. Bowmer, *Sacrament*, 29.

allegiance to the new king and queen on the religious grounds of divine right of succession. A number of bishops and hundreds of priests were removed from their posts but continued in their own commitment to the "apostolic succession." This group took on new life as soon as it coalesced. This became much more than a matter of ascendancy to the throne; it was an intricate mixture of political and theological issues. According to Robert Cornwall:

> Had William been content with a regency, the nonjuring schism would never have occurred, but his demand for the crown caused a significant disturbance within the established Church of England. Many Church of England clergy held a strict doctrine of divine right monarchy, and while the majority found ways of accommodating the changes, the change in monarchs placed these clergy in a difficult situation. Most of those who would become Nonjurors had opposed James' pro-Catholic policies and were concerned about the future of the Church of England should he remain on the throne. They could not, however, recognize as legitimate the change of monarchs.[5]

The revolution that swept William and Mary into power made room for "low-church" theologians called "Latitudinarians" (allowing for "latitude") to emerge in England. While most nonjuring bishops who opposed his ascendancy were Scottish, the new King William had Calvinist leanings. So he reinstated Presbyterianism as the established church in Scotland.[6] Cornwall writes, "The archbishop of Canterbury, together with seven other bishops and four hundred clergy were evicted from their places in church and state, while the episcopal Church of Scotland, upon its refusal to recognize William and Mary's claim to the throne, was disestablished and replaced with the Presbyterians."[7]

Subjects that were loyal to James II and opposed to William and Mary were eventually called Jacobites ("Jacobus" is the Latin form of James). They included Catholics, dissenters against these

---

5. Cornwall, "Theologies of the Nonjurors," 2.
6. Hefling, "Episcopalians and Nonjurors," 168–69.
7. Cornwall, "Theologies of the Nonjurors," 2.

The Mystery of Presence

Presbyterians, and conservative Anglicans. This last group, the conservative Anglicans, basically constituted the Nonjurors which influenced Wesley so much. Cornwall says, "They were a distinctly high church movement that placed episcopacy at the heart of the Anglican tradition. They were also determined advocates of a high church political theology that insisted on divine right monarchy."[8] In time, the Nonjurors began to take on a theological distinctiveness. Cornwall says:

> As a Counter-Enlightenment movement the Nonjurors sought to reclaim the past in order to counter the inroads of what they considered a radical new theology and its underlying philosophy. Initially the partisans of the nonjuring movement focused on defending the ousted bishops for refusing to take the oaths, but in time those in the movement who did not return to the fold moved onto other substantive and theological issues.[9]

The Longing for "Primitive" Christianity

With that background, we can explore what became characteristic of the Communion theology of the Nonjurors that influenced Wesley. It began with the freedom—which the separation from the established church brought—from conforming to the 1662 Book of Common Prayer. Little by little, they introduced variations in the Communion liturgy.[10] This came from a longing for the spirituality of the early church. Cornwall describes it as an impulse that led them to search early church sources: "The Nonjuror program was primitivist in orientation. They sought the restoration of the ancient church in British form. Not content with either the Protestant or Catholic versions of the Christian faith, as the schism wore

---

8. Cornwall, "Theologies of the Nonjurors," 1.
9. Cornwall, "Theologies of the Nonjurors," 4.
10. Hefling, "Episcopalians and Nonjurors," 170.

on, they became more and more enamored with the idea that they could restore the ancient church."[11]

There it is. Plumbing the depths of history, they discovered that the early church seemed to consider Christ as *present* in the Communion gathering in mysterious ways. This presence was not about the elements (the substance of the bread and wine being transformed), but this was so much more than memorializing Jesus. Their search for these ancient practices brought them to what they called the four "usages." These were four ancient elements of the liturgy that were missing and needed reclaiming.[12]

One was the mixed chalice (putting a little water in the wine), and a second was the prayer for the dead. The third was the epiclesis (a prayer invoking the Holy Spirit over the bread and cup), and fourth was the prayer of "oblation" offering the bread and wine as a sacrifice to God. While some Nonjurors simply preferred the earlier 1549 liturgy over the 1662 version in the Book of Common Prayer, Nonjurors such as Thomas Brett and Thomas Deacon experimented with new liturgies that made room for these four usages. Cornwall adds, "While most Nonjurors believed that the four usages were desirable they did not believe them to be either necessary or practical. This sentiment was especially strong among those who held out hope of reunion with the larger church. Brett and Deacon, however, believed that not only was the existing liturgy deficient[,] it did not properly convey saving grace."[13] Liturgies they wrote in 1718 and 1734 are great examples of Nonjuror Communion theology, though they were never widely used.[14]

Before we get lost on a road trip through these Nonjuror liturgies, let us decide it is well beyond the scope of this book. I would like to draw us back to our purpose, which is to see where the theme of "real" presence appears in the spirituality of John Wesley. Henry Broxap says what is most curious about the Communion theology of the later Nonjurors is how elaborate their explanation was of

11. Cornwall, "Theologies of the Nonjurors," 5.
12. Hammond, "High Church Anglican Influences," 188.
13. Cornwall, "Theologies of the Nonjurors," 6.
14. Cornwall, "Theologies of the Nonjurors," 6.

their doctrine of the real presence of Christ in the sacrament. For them, when the priest says the words "this is my body" and "this is my blood," the *effect* of the words is that they become signs of Christ's body and blood. They are then offered to God, who accepts the sacrifice and returns it again for us to feast on. The bread and cup are made the spiritual, life-giving body of Christ in *power* and in *virtue*, or quality.[15] So to say that the presence of Christ in the sacrament is in "virtue, power, and effect" is to dismiss the Catholic teaching of transubstantiation, the idea that the bread and wine have been transformed in some way. Broxap spots this teaching in a letter of Bishop Thomas Brett to his friend Campbell, written in 1728 or 1729: "We do adore Him. We draw near to the Holy Table or Altar with reverence and worship Him Whom we believe invisibly yet in a more especial manner present there . . . spiritually and sacramentally present though not corporally."[16]

For the Nonjurors, the real presence of Christ is more than a spiritual sense inside the heart of a believer. Something *real* happens, and it has power for something to *really* happen to us. This may be why Communion was celebrated by Nonjurors more frequently than other Anglican clergy of the time, and for some, it was observed weekly on Sundays.[17]

Wesley's Personal Connections with Nonjurors

Let us now turn to John Wesley's personal connection with Nonjurors. Wesley had a personal relationship with a few, including Thomas Deacon, who was a close friend of someone in Wesley's Holy Club.[18] Bowmer adds that "all Wesley's customs, as recorded by himself and imputed to him by his accusers, confirm the conclusion that his aim in Georgia was to regulate his Church by the

---

15. Broxap, *Later Non-jurors*, 318–19.
16. Thomas Brett, qtd. in Broxap, *Later Non-jurors*, 321.
17. Broxap, *Later Non-jurors*, 329.
18. Bowmer, *Sacrament*, 26–28.

ideals of the Nonjurors."[19] In later chapters, we will pick up on the way two of the four usages, the epiclesis (prayer to the Holy Spirit) and the prayer offering the bread and wine to God, were adopted by Wesley. But let us begin with Wesley and this essential concept of the mystery of Christ's presence. For Wesley, something real happens at the Lord's Supper, and it constitutes the presence of Christ in "virtue, power, and effect."

John Wesley traveled to Georgia to become chaplain of the relatively new Oglethorpe settlement in 1735. Seeing Georgia as a laboratory for implementing his vision of primitive Christianity, his focus was on liturgical purity and holy living.[20] The Nonjuror emphasis on sacraments and the teachings of the early church really resonated with Wesley. The Nonjuror liturgies published by Brett and Deacon came out just as Wesley was preparing to go to Georgia in 1735. According to Hammond, this controversy was absorbed by Wesley, who went beyond what he was authorized to do by employing the four "usages" discussed above in the colony: "In the Eucharist he mixed water with wine in the sacramental cup . . . and altered the Book of Common Prayer's communion liturgy to bring it into agreement with the usages."[21]

The Nonjurors appealed to Wesley's fascination with the primitive church. In the year of the death of his father, Samuel, John Wesley published a pamphlet based on a manuscript Samuel had sent him a decade earlier. About half of the pamphlet was on what young clergy should study, including early church teachers such as Ignatius and Athanasius.[22] In his journals, Wesley quotes Anglican scholars who studied early church theologians, for they appealed to Wesley as he went to the laboratory of the Georgia colony.[23]

Wesley's connection with the Nonjurors was more than theological. It was also quite a family matter. His father, Samuel, saw James II as a tyrant, but his mother, Susanna, supported the

---

19. Bowmer, *Sacrament*, 36.
20. Hammond, "High Church Anglican Influences," 175.
21. Hammond, "High Church Anglican Influences," 176.
22. Hammond, "High Church Anglican Influences," 177–78.
23. Hammond, "High Church Anglican Influences," 183.

The Mystery of Presence

king. There was a Wesley family quarrel in 1702, just before John was born and after the death of James II. Susanna refused to say "Amen" to Samuel's prayers for William and Mary, and he refused to have physical relations with her until she asked for God's forgiveness. A few years later, Samuel gave up. Susanna's surviving letters regarding this indicate her relationships with Nonjurors. One letter received a reply from George Hickes, a Nonjuror, who urged her to obey her conscience and criticized Samuel for not fulfilling his wedding vows.[24]

John Wesley's adult life was, of course, farther removed from this conflict over William and Mary, but this Nonjuror influence instilled in him a love for the primitive church.[25] Later Nonjurors began focusing on additional theological issues. Hammond believes they increasingly began to argue that the 1549 Book of Common Prayer needed to be supplemented with primitive liturgies and prayers that were apostolic in origin. This created a "pamphlet war" between Usagers and Non-usagers. Wesley was aware of this, for Hammond notes that "as Wesley remarked on his return trip from Georgia, the Usagers made 'antiquity a co-ordinate (rather than a subordinate) rule with scriptures,' a theological claim he did not dispute."[26] In his journal upon returning to England from Georgia in 1737, Wesley referred to "Essentialist" Nonjurors whose vision for restoring early-church Christianity he had adopted for his mission to Georgia.[27] Hammond notes that Wesley "drew on the *Constitutions*,[28] the Apostolic Canons (eighty-five teachings attributed to the apostles that form the final chapter of the *Constitutions*), and Deacon's *Devotions*

---

24. Hammond, "High Church Anglican Influences," 179.
25. Hammond, "High Church Anglican Influences," 187.
26. Hammond, "High Church Anglican Influences," 188–89.
27. Hammond, "High Church Anglican Influences," 193.
28. The *Apostolic Constitutions* are traditionally attributed to Clement of Alexandria or Clement of Rome, and it is believed he compiled them from earlier oral traditions passed on by the apostles. Though modern scholars date them later, they were a revered source of primitive liturgy for Nonjurors (Hammond, "High Church Anglican Influences," 189–91).

to compose a series of resolutions that he observed in Georgia, including a commitment to observe the four usages."[29]

The evidence of usages in Wesley's early ministry is clear. The Eucharist as an offering representing Christ's sacrifice is a prominent theme in the Wesley brothers' Communion hymns.[30] A commitment to pray for the dead is in Wesley's 1733 *Collection of Forms of Prayer*; in a letter, he notes his commitment to commune in a church with a chalice of wine mixed with water. Two years later, these three usages, and the fourth usage of the prayer invoking the Holy Spirit, are all explicitly listed as duties to observe in Wesley's resolutions for his practice in Georgia.[31]

In the next chapter on anamnesis, or remembrance, we will consider Wesley's adoption of offering language in Wesleyan Communion hymns. There seems to be no evidence that prayer for the dead and the mixed chalice remained in Wesleyan practice later in his life and ministry, but the theme of offering stays deeply imbedded in Wesleyan Communion hymns. The epiclesis—the prayer to the Holy Spirit—also came to be a distinctive element in Methodist sacramental thought.

But of the three major emphases of the Nonjurors that influenced Wesley (the quest for recovering primitive Christianity, the four usages, and the doctrine of real presence through "virtue, power, and effect"), it is important for our journey to focus on the third major influence, the doctrine of Christ's presence, which permeates Wesleyan Communion theology. It is no wonder that we feel Christ's presence in our Communion gatherings still today.

---

29. Hammond, "High Church Anglican Influences," 199.

30. Wesley and Wesley, *Lord's Supper*. The first of six sections groups hymns under the category "*As it is a Memorial of the Sufferings and Death of CHRIST*" and includes hymns prominently featuring this theme of sacrifice and oblation. This will be discussed at length below.

31. Hammond, "High Church Anglican Influences," 202.

The Mystery of Presence

The "Duty of Constant Communion"

Like Nonjurors, Wesley was a firm believer in frequent Communion, and there is evidence that he had practiced a weekly Eucharist since as early as 1725. This was unusual for Anglicans at the time, when sharing Communion four times per year was common. The stress on frequent Communion was maintained long after his missionary work was complete,[32] and it was a prominent theme in his sermon "The Duty of Constant Communion," where Wesley says, "This is the food of our souls: this gives strength to perform our duty, and leads us on to perfection. If therefore we have any regard for the plain command of Christ, if we desire the pardon for our sins, if we wish for strength to believe, to love and obey God, then we should neglect no opportunity of receiving the Lord's Supper."[33] This sermon hints at the power and effect of divine presence in the table's "strengthening and refreshing of our souls."[34]

Hammond notes that there is evidence in Wesley's journal of the influence of Nonjuror John Johnson, including *The Unbloody Sacrifice*. Johnson saw the power and effect of the sacrifice as flowing from the original sacrifice of Christ, who is not present in the elements themselves but is nevertheless personally present in virtue. This was not what is called a "receptionist" doctrine, since the consecration was not dependent on the heart of the individual.[35] Hammond points out that while most Anglican clergy of the time held to the theology of the 1662 Prayer Book, with a "memorialist" doctrine of sacrifice and a "receptionist" view of presence, Wesley in Georgia practiced belief in a real presence through the action of the Holy Spirit, by whom the bread and wine become the body and blood *in effect*.[36]

In 1732, there is an exchange of letters between John Wesley and his mother, Susanna, in which they both affirm the presence

---

32. Bowmer, *Sacrament*, 55–56.
33. Outler and Heitzenrater, *John Wesley's Sermons*, 503.
34. Outler and Heitzenrater, *John Wesley's Sermons*, 502.
35. Hammond, "Wesleys' Sacramental Theology," 53–54.
36. Hammond, "Wesleys' Sacramental Theology," 59.

of Christ in Communion. Susanna wrote a concise expression of this doctrine of presence: "Surely the divine presence of our Lord, thus applying the virtue and merits of the great atonement to each believer, makes the consecrated bread more than a bare sign of Christ's body, since by his so doing we receive, not only the sign, but with it the thing signified—all of the benefits of his Incarnation and Passion."[37] Wesley's doctrine of Communion as a "converting ordinance" downplays the significance of "worthy" reception. With the Nonjurors, Wesley linked Christ's presence in Communion not with the reception of the heart but with the Spirit's role, invoked in the prayer to the Holy Spirit.[38]

Wesley's theology of Communion regarding Christ's presence did not change over his lifetime.[39] Some might imagine that after Wesley's iconic, heartwarming Aldersgate experience, his high-church leanings were transformed into low-church preferences, but that is simply not the case. In early American Methodist society meetings, field preaching, establishing of churches, and licensing of local pastors, there was a lack of formality in atmosphere, but there was no watering down of sacramental theology. The stress was on God's action invoked in the prayer to the Holy Spirit. The early American missionary organization of ordained elders who supervised local pastors and who brought the sacraments into the pastor's parish upon their visit maintained the sense of Christ's presence for a people who were hungry for it.[40]

---

37. Hammond, "Wesleys' Sacramental Theology," 60.

38. Hammond, "Wesley's Sacramental Theology," 65. "Converting ordinance" is Wesley's phrase.

39. S T Kimbrough, Jr., preface to the facsimile reprint of Wesley and Wesley, *Lord's Supper*, iii. Kimbrough notes that Wesleyan eucharistic hymns went through nine editions, with few substantive changes, during the Wesley brothers' lifetimes.

40. Hammond, "Wesley's Sacramental Theology, " 65–67.

The Mystery of Presence

"Real" Presence in Hymns and Writings

There is quite a bit of reference to the mystery of presence in various hymns and written works of the Wesley brothers. In the collection *Hymns on the Lord's Supper* published with John's brother Charles, John includes as a preface his abridgment of *The Christian Sacrament and Sacrifice* by Daniel Brevint. Brevint says it well: "At the Holy Table the People meet to worship GOD, and GOD is present, to meet and bless his People."[41] This theme is carried into Wesleyan hymns. One of them sings:

> Come dear Redeemer of Mankind,
>   We long thy Open Face to see,
> Appear, and all who seek shall find
>   Their Bliss consummated in Thee.
>
> Thy Presence shall the Cloud dispart,
>   Thy Presence shall the Life display,
> Then, then our All in all Thou art,
>   Our Fullness of Eternal Day.[42]

The presence of Christ is very real for the Wesleys. Christ is with us when we gather! Another hymn sings, "Come, Thou Witness of his Dying, / Come, Remembrancer Divine, / Let us feel thy Power applying / CHRIST to every Soul and mine."[43] And yet another sings:

> SINNER with Awe draw near,
>   And find thy Saviour here,
>   In his Ordinances still,
>   Touch his Sacramental Cloaths,
>   Present in his Power to heal,
>   Virtue from his Body flows.[44]

---

41. Daniel Brevint, preface to Wesley and Wesley, *Lord's Supper*, 3. Note that texts will be cited just as the Wesley brothers included them in the first edition of the collection. Unusual spelling as well as capitalization and italicizing of words for emphasis will be unaltered.

42. Wesley and Wesley, *Lord's Supper*, 29.

43. Wesley and Wesley, *Lord's Supper*, 13.

44. Wesley and Wesley, *Lord's Supper*, 29.

Something Happens Here

The spiritual reality of Christ's presence, for Wesley, dwells with and in us. This has a purifying effect. Another hymn sings:

> SAVIOUR, and can it be
>   That Thou should dwell with me!
> From thy high and lofty Throne,
>   Throne of Everlasting Bliss,
> Will thy Majesty stoop down
>   To so mean an House as This?
>
> I am not worthy, LORD,
>   So foul, so self-abhor'd,
> Thee, my GOD, to entertain
>   In this poor polluted Heart:
> I am a frail Sinful Man,
>   All my Nature cries, depart!
>
> Yet come Thou heavenly Guest,
>   And purify my Breast,
> Come Thou great and glorious King,
>   While before thy Cross I bow,
> With Thyself Salvation bring,
>   Cleanse the House by entering Now.[45]

Another hymn sings, "Visit us in Pard'ning Grace, / CHRIST the Crucified appear, / Come in thy Appointed Ways, / Come, and meet, and bless us here."[46] Perhaps most obviously, the sense of presence is in the final verse of this Wesley hymn:

> We need not now go up to Heaven
>   To bring the long-sought Saviour down,
> Thou art to All already given:
>   Thou dost ev'n Now thy Banquet crown,
> To every faithful Soul appear,
>   And shew thy Real Presence here.[47]

We will look at more of the Wesleys' hymns in later chapters. But it should be clear by now that Wesley adopted the Nonjuror

---

45. Wesley and Wesley, *Lord's Supper*, 32.
46. Wesley and Wesley, *Lord's Supper*, 47.
47. Wesley and Wesley, *Lord's Supper*, 99.

The Mystery of Presence

understanding of Christ's presence in "virtue, power, and effect" in his theology.

Wesley did not believe the presence of Christ was in the bread itself, and he clarifies that position on the disputes of their time. In his *Explanatory Notes upon the New Testament*, he wrote regarding Luke 22:19 with his usual wit: "As he had just now celebrated the paschal supper, which was called the Passover, so, in the like figurative language, he calls this bread his body. And this circumstance of itself was sufficient to prevent any mistake, as if this bread was his real body, any more than the paschal lamb was really the Passover." Wesley also wrote, regarding verse 20, "Here is an undeniable figure, whereby the cup is put for the wine in the cup. And this is called, The New Testament in Christ's blood, which could not possibly mean, that it was the New Testament itself, but only the seal of it, and the sign of the blood which was shed to confirm it."[48]

Christ wasn't in the bread or cup, yet for Wesley, Christ is present nevertheless. Geoffrey Wainwright notes that Wesley follows Brevint's lead in his "high view of the sacramental presence of Christ."[49] To put it simply, Jesus shows up when we gather at the table. For Wesley, Christ's presence is real, and it's in the gathering of the people around the table of grace. Wesley would agree with what Gordon Lathrop says about the church as *ecclesia*, the New Testament Greek word for the church which refers to the gathering, and his idea that the "assembly, a gathering together of participating persons, constitutes the most basic symbol of Christian worship. All the other symbols and symbolic actions of liturgy depend upon this gathering being there in the first place."[50] Bruce Morrill adds, "We must not lose sight of the humbling fact that such ritualizing—the doing of liturgy—is the human action of a divinely assembled body of human beings. This liturgical reality is humbling because it confronts us with the revelation of how far

---

48. Wesley, *Explanatory Notes*, 245–46.

49. Geoffrey Wainwright, introduction to Wesley and Wesley, *Lord's Supper*, vii.

50. Lathrop, *Holy People*, 21.

and wide and deep the self-emptying love of God in Christ continues to reach through space and time."[51]

Morrill also notes that the presence of Christ is "hidden amid the church's assembly and diffused through its members in the world."[52] Lathrop puts this truth simply in saying that "the church is the assembly. It is the people who cannot be the holy people, and yet, because of Christ, *are*."[53] Wesley and the Nonjurors would agree. They would say this is, indeed, because of the quality, the power, and the effect of Christ's presence. As the Wesleys succinctly sang, "O, taste and see that God is here."[54]

Real Presence in Times of Real Division

This makes a difference as we look to the future of the church, whatever is being reborn. As I write, the United States is reeling in the aftermath of the infamous failed insurrection against our nation's capital led by a group of anarchists, white supremacists, and supporters of conspiracy theories seeking to overturn presidential election results. This happened after an unprecedented global pandemic created heightened levels of diffuse anxiety across the world, and at the same time violence against African Americans exposed deep divides over systemic racism lingering in our nation. We are acutely aware of the level of political division in our country, and this divisiveness has spilled over into the church. Those making plans to withdraw from the United Methodist Church have announced the launch of a new denomination, tired of navigating the diversity of thought within the United Methodist Church.

Communion "reminds us to remember" that these culture wars did not originate within the church; they are a *fundamental threat* to our true identity. Our table gatherings explicitly stand against this divisiveness—not because we agree on every matter

---

51. Morrill, *Encountering Christ*, 36.
52. Morrill, *Encountering Christ*, 45.
53. Lathrop, *Holy People*, 18.
54. Wesley and Wesley, *Lord's Supper*, 8.

The Mystery of Presence

but because Christ shows his real presence here. It is not for us to decide who may or may not come to the table or who is affirmed and who is merely tolerated. Deeming broad categories of people as unfit to preside at the table, regardless of God's calling on their lives, their pastoral effectiveness, or the cultural context, is telling. For Wesley, the presence of Christ is not located in the bread, or in the celebrant, or even in the words of the liturgy. It's in the gathering.

Communion is not a dry ritual that is about hurrying through what is printed in the hymnal rather than beholding the vast mystery in the room, and it is not simply a divine snack to hold us over until next time. It is not an object lesson we use to teach a principle or a doctrine, nor is it some kind of spiritual vending machine we use to exchange confession for forgiveness so that we, as consumers, can get back to our regular lives. The table is our *life*, because when we gather there, Christ is there. He is the light that glows like candles in our circle of prayer.

Christ is not lying on the table, resting in the cup, or hiding under the napkin; he's present in our midst because we are his gathered body, redeemed by his blood. Experiencing his presence in us and among us must change the way we see everything about our life together as a church. Being in community is messy, but that's the very nature of love. In a time when we seem to be increasingly focused on disagreements over who can come to the table, what it means to be welcomed, and who we will and will not remain in communion with, it is easy to forget *whose* table it is. Something happens here. We cannot really be a holy people, and yet we *are* . . . because of Christ, who binds us together no matter what threatens to drive us apart.

3

Experiencing Anew

ONE OF MY DEAR childhood memories is of playing with my Granny's boxes. Granny Hamby lived in a "superannuate home" for clergy and surviving spouses, an apartment provided by the North Alabama Conference in a suburb of Birmingham called Fairfield, Alabama. By the time I came along, her preacher husband had been deceased for about fifteen years.

It's strange that there are only two things I remember about her retirement apartment. The first is the light-gray carpet in her living room, complete with an indented paisley pattern in it that I could trace with my fingers. And the other thing I remember are the boxes she let me play on that carpet with.

I don't know how often it happened, and I don't know if the particular boxes etched in my memory were refrigerator boxes or for some other appliance. What I do remember is that they were big (at least to me at ages four and five) and they led to endless, playful imagination. In Granny's living room, I could set up forts, castles, or tunnels and pretend that the indentions in the carpet were part of a moat or river. I could craft the design of my latest adventure, crawl through that world, and then do it all over again.

Experiencing Anew

We learn best by experiencing. I had, of course, heard stories about King Arthur, cowboys and Indians, and cavemen, and I had seen pictures. Those are forms of learning. But to play is to grow, to become, to interact with a story. These boxes were among my first workshops for learning all there was to learn about life.

As I have grown older, I've realized that one of the best ways to learn is to experience and reexperience what I'm learning about. When I lead confirmation classes for young people, I refuse to have them just sit in a classroom and write things on the board. I take them on field trips, great and small, even around the building. My favorite session is our visit to the ancient catacombs (usually simulated in the basement of the church somewhere) to experience early church worship in times of persecution and learn about the deepest roots of Christian symbolism. We learn by engaging, by seeing, by touching, and by doing.

In the expansive wisdom of God, in Communion we were given a gift of engaging the grace that we profess. It's something we do with Christ and each other—or better yet, it's something Christ does *with* us and not just *for* us. Communion is not just a cognitive reminder of the meaning of the sacrifice of Christ that saves us from sin (if a reminder is all we need, a few well-crafted bullet points would do).

But Jesus said, "Do this in remembrance of me."[1] He did not say, "Don't forget what this means." *Do this.* Communion is most definitely not playacting, but it's much more than recalling something with our brains. It is experiencing something with our entire being, reexperiencing the multivalent narrative of the Lord's Supper in ways that bring freshness to the senses and engage the whole self.

Let us return for a moment to the prism on my bookshelf. If the white light that pours through is the light of Christ's presence, then if you hold the glass up to that light and turn it a bit, it illuminates color that wasn't quite distinguishable before. I suggest that's what Wesley did. In the previous chapter, we looked at his teaching regarding the mystery of the "sure and real"[2] presence

---

1. Luke 22:19.
2. "Sure and real" is a phrase we will use from one of Wesley's hymns

of Christ in the gathered community. I proposed that this idea of presence, gleaned from early Christian history through the eyes of the Nonjurors, shines through the prism in three distinct ways, as the colors of life and love become evident in Wesley's eucharistic thought. This chapter explores the first of these, the language of sacrifice and offering in John and Charles Wesley's Communion hymns. For Wesley, at the Communion table we are *experiencing anew* the sacrificial offering of Christ in our *present* offering of our liturgy, and life, at the table.

Remembrance of Christ's Sacrifice

Let us have a look at the New Testament Greek term *anamnesis*. Usually translated "remembrance" in relaying the words of Jesus at the table, a good look at this word will help us bring to light this special feature of Wesleyan Communion spirituality. Again, the Gospels report that Jesus said, "Do this in remembrance of me." Remembrance is more than reminiscing; this can be lost when we think of "doing this in remembrance" of Jesus as recalling details and facts in order to "understand" its "meaning." Anamnesis challenges us because it is not about bringing memories to *mind*. It is about bringing memory to *life* and bringing life to memory.

The Greek word *anamnesis* appears in the versions of the institution of Holy Communion recorded in 1 Corinthians and Luke.[3] Of course, we do not know the exact phrasing uttered from Christ's lips in his Galilean tongue of Jewish Aramaic, but in the New Testament account, the Greek *anamnesis* was used. I believe the translation "recollection" is better than "remembrance," because anamnesis does exactly that. It collects together again ancient memory and contemporary experience; it is a coming together of timeless truth and momentary taste and touch. It is an act of "re-membering," or putting the pieces (the "members") together again. Communion is not a memorial to a past event (that would

(Wesley and Wesley, *Lord's Supper*, 41).

3. It is usually translated "remembrance" in 1 Cor 11:24–25 and Luke 22:19.

be like a "funeral" for Jesus), nor is it simply an object lesson to teach a conceptual truth (that Jesus died for our sins). Remembrance brings all things together in the spirit of Christ, who said, "And I, when I am lifted up from the earth, will draw all people to myself."[4] Communion is like a magnet drawing together historical events, the salvation narrative, comprehensive theology, human experience, and the struggles and joys of life in the body of Christ. It gives a pattern to the pieces. It is a refreshing rediscovery of the knowledge already within us.

This idea of bringing memory to life, and life to memory, is as ancient as Communion itself. Anamnesis appears in a number of ancient liturgies of the early church. An example is the liturgy of Saint John Chrysostom, which reads: "*(Silently)* We therefore, remembering this saving commandment and all the things that were done for us: the cross, the tomb, the resurrection on the third day, the ascension into heaven, the session at the right hand, the second and glorious coming again; *(aloud)* offering you your own from your own, in all and for all, *(people)* we hymn you." "We hymn you" is an ancient liturgical phrase meaning to "bless you" and "give you thanks."[5]

Anamnesis, however, is not just a phrase in the liturgy (one of the "parts") but a theology of the whole. It is beyond the scope of this book to cover the breadth of either historical or contemporary theology of how anamnesis is seen (and where the "moment," so to speak, of consecration happens in the liturgy), but generally speaking, there is a contemporary realization among theologians that the entire prayer is what consecrates. The various formulas within the prayers do not consecrate Communion. The whole experience does. I would add that the whole experience, then, is the anamnesis. Jesus said, "Do this [*all* of this, not just these words or this ritual] in remembrance of me." Remembrance is bringing memory to life in a vibrant faith community so we are living and practicing what it is we remember.

4. John 12:32.
5. Bradshaw and Johnson, *Eucharistic Liturgies*, 99–100. Parenthetical notes and italics in the original.

Something Happens Here

In the Gospels of Matthew, Mark, and Luke, the holy meal occurs in the context of a Passover celebration. The simple phrases "While they were eating, Jesus took a loaf of bread"[6] and "He did the same with the cup after supper"[7] remind us of the fullness of liturgical action around the meal shared during the night. The actions of Jesus himself, which are to take, bless, break, and give, are meaningful gestures that have formed countless devotions. There were multiple blessing prayers in the Passover, as "a *berakah* (a blessing of God) was to be said before anything was consumed."[8]

So it greatly undercuts the power of the Communion experience to treat it is an object lesson or teaching moment about the "meaning" of sin and forgiveness. Jesus drew the symbolism of Passover into himself, and he drew himself into the symbol of the table. Again, he said to do this "in remembrance of *me*," not of this *ritual*. Passover symbolism was all redirected to the person of Jesus. Remembrance is being drawn into a timeless, ongoing, experiential journey of deliverance through Christ. Anamnesis is about the entire experience, and it transforms us. God is so gracious as to continue to form this community as the body of Christ, redeemed by his blood. We do not *reenact* these events in history. We *reexperience* them in a way that "recollects," or draws together, our story with God's story, our past and our future. Remembrance is not "the problem of how people can connect to a past event but rather the challenge of how to live the reality the commemoration actualizes among them."[9]

The importance of this discussion of anamnesis for our purposes is that we can clearly see evidence of the Wesley brothers' attempts to bring anamnesis to bear in the life of the community. They do this through their eucharistic hymns, for they assist the worshiper to relive the memory, not simply recall it. As Bruce Morrill has said, "Repetition connects generations of followers to the Lord's promised presence in the command 'Do this in memory

---

6. Matt 26:26.
7. Luke 22:20.
8. Morrill, *Encountering Christ*, 85. Parenthetical note in the original.
9. Morrill, *Encountering Christ*, 89.

Experiencing Anew

of me.'"[10] For Wesley, his Communion theology brings memory to life in numerous references to the imagery of sacrifice. Let us look at Wesley's use of this biblical language. For Wesley, we reexperience the sacrifice of Christ when we offer ourselves to God.

I should pause to say that the Communion hymns of the Wesleys contain extensive use of the themes of sacrifice and offering, though this theme is not particularly evident in Wesley's sermons, journal notes, and writings (a love for the table most certainly was). Yet, "Once this small book of hymns was issued, it became and remained the Wesley's principal statement of their sacramental doctrine and spirituality . . . the *Hymns on the Lord's Supper* went through nine editions during his lifetime, with only unimportant changes."[11]

Daniel Brevint's Influence on the Wesleys' Communion Hymns

The first thing to notice is John Wesley's inclusion of the work of Daniel Brevint, a Nonjuror referenced in the previous chapter. Assuming John was the principal editor,[12] it is a potent statement that an abridgment of Brevint's work was included at the beginning of the Wesley brothers' book of Communion hymns. This abridgment, one-third of the original length of the 1673 version authored by Brevint, represented "sharp dissent" from Roman Catholic doctrine of transubstantiation, the idea that the bread and cup are changed.[13] Brevint makes a clear statement of his alternative view of anamnesis: "This Sacrament duly receiv'd, makes

---

10. Morrill, *Encountering Christ*, 83.

11. Stevick, *Altar's Fire*, 5. This echoes Kimbrough's observations cited earlier in Wesley and Wesley, *Lord's Supper*, iii.

12. It is generally assumed that Charles Wesley was the primary hymn text writer and John Wesley the primary editor, based on general knowledge of the Wesleys. The volume itself does not make a distinction between the two.

13. Stevick, *Altar's Fire*, 21–25.

the thing which it represents, as really present for our Use, as if it were newly done."[14]

In fact, Wesley's arrangement of the hymns into sections reflects an adaption of Brevint's writing, and the section titles are revealing in themselves:

1. As it is a Memorial of the Sufferings and Death of CHRIST.[15]
2. As it is a Sign and a Means of Grace.[16]
3. The SACRAMENT a Pledge of HEAVEN.[17]
4. The HOLY EUCHARIST as it implies a Sacrifice.[18]
5. Concerning the Sacrifice of our Persons.[19]
6. After the SACRAMENT.[20]

In this chapter on anamnesis as experiencing anew the sacrifice of Christ, we will explore a few of the hymns in sections 1, 4, and 5 and return to other sections later. These three sections contain hymns on the themes of Christ's sacrifice and our sacrificial offering. The very first hymn in the whole collection, before including the words of institution, emphasizes how this memorial expresses a deeper love which comes alive in our present offering:

> He took, and bless'd, and brake the Bread,
> And gave his Own their last Bequest,
> And thus his Love's Intent exprest:
> Take, eat, this is my Body, given,
>   To purchase Life and Peace for You,
> Pardon and Holiness in Heaven;
>   Do this, my dying Love to shew,
> Accept your precious Legacy,

14. Daniel Brevint, preface to Wesley and Wesley, *Lord's Supper*, 5.
15. Wesley and Wesley, *Lord's Supper*, 1.
16. Wesley and Wesley, *Lord's Supper*, 22.
17. Wesley and Wesley, *Lord's Supper*, 81.
18. Wesley and Wesley, *Lord's Supper*, 98.
19. Wesley and Wesley, *Lord's Supper*, 109.
20. Wesley and Wesley, *Lord's Supper*, 132.

Experiencing Anew

And thus, my Friends, remember me.[21]

The second hymn makes references to wheat and fire in the bread itself, symbols of how the bread "suffered" as Christ did, "And lo! my LORD is here become / The bread of Life to me!"[22] Including the words "to me" points to Wesley's sense of anamnesis as bringing to our experience the sacrifice of Christ in our present offering. A third hymn sings, "But JESU'S death is ever New," and continues:

> Th' Oblation sends as sweet a Smell,
> Even now it pleases GOD as well
>   As when it first was made;
> The Blood doth now as freely flow,
> As when his Side receiv'd the Blow
>   That shew'd him newly dead.
>
> Then let our Faith adore the Lamb
> To day as yesterday the same,
>   In thy great Offering join . . .[23]

For Wesley, when we come to the table in our present experience, we are joining in the "great offering." Our offerings of the bread and cup at the table do not perform the work of sacrifice again and again, for the saving work of Christ was done *once* for all time. However, Communion brings this sacrifice to *life*. We are joining ourselves to it. Again, in the fourth hymn:

> And still we by his Death are blest,
>   And share his Sacrifice.
> By Faith his Flesh we eat,
>   Who here his Passion shew,
> And GOD out of his Holy Seat
>   Shall all his Gifts bestow.[24]

---

21. Wesley and Wesley, *Lord's Supper*, 1–2.
22. Wesley and Wesley, *Lord's Supper*, 3. This book will note in a subsequent chapter how this imagery preceded Wesley in both the *Didache* and in the eucharistic sermons of Augustine.
23. Wesley and Wesley, *Lord's Supper*, 4.
24. Wesley and Wesley, *Lord's Supper*, 4.

The fifth and eighth hymns in the collection note how our participation keeps the one-time offering of Christ very much alive and fresh in our experience, in that "Thy Offering still continues New, / Thy Vesture keeps its Bloody Hue."[25] And:

> In this Authentic Sign
>   Behold the Stamp Divine:
> CHRIST revives his Sufferings here,
>   Still exposes them to View . . .[26]

The Lord's Supper "revives" and "exposes" the love of Christ. For Wesley, this is not simply recalling a past event but a remembrance, a "coming alive," of the sacrificial love of Christ in the present moment. Hymns eleven and thirteen sing:

> Come then our Dying LORD,
>   To Us thy Goodness shew,
> In Honour of thy Word
>   The Inward Grace bestow.
>
> His Blood which once for All atones,
>   And brings us *now* to GOD.[27]

Daniel Stevick describes the memorial section of the Wesley hymns as leading to a "deeply involved beholder." We are drawn into the experience of Christ's offering of himself: "A believer cannot look at the cross and remain a disinterested observer; one is drawn into the event." This section of hymns expresses a sense that Communion creates drama between the believer and the Holy Spirit.[28] Is this not anamnesis? Communion is not simply coming to the table out of obedience. It is a place of interactive presence, of Christ, whose love is experienced anew as we become more present to God. In a hymn in one of the later sections of the collection, we sing:

> As Incense to thy Throne above,
>   O let our Prayers arise

---

25. Wesley and Wesley, *Lord's Supper*, 5.
26. Wesley and Wesley, *Lord's Supper*, 7.
27. Wesley and Wesley, *Lord's Supper*, 10–11.
28. Stevick, *Altar's Fire*, 66.

Experiencing Anew

>   Wing with thy Flames of Holy Love
>   Our living Sacrifice.[29]

Our offering is only *effective* to the extent that it is *enlivened* by the love of Christ, which gives it "wings." The movement of grace is toward *us*, as the Wesleys sang: "In thine Ordinance be near us."[30] At times, our contemporary ears might find Wesley's descriptions of the sacrifice of Christ distasteful, as in "See his Body mangled, rent, / Cover'd with a gore of Blood!"[31] Yuck. But there is a real sense in which we are drawn into his sacrifice—"And stand in all thy Wounds confest, / And wrap us in thy Bloody Vest"—as we claim "Our Share in thy great Sacrifice."[32]

These hymns from the Wesleys bring the language of sacrifice to life and clarify that *our* offering does not repeat the saving power of Christ's love at the cross. In discussing the offering in Methodist liturgy, Dick Eslinger writes, "The offertory, for Luther, is to be purged of all that 'smacks' of sacrifice and priestly offering which, he insists, is a blatant example of works righteousness."[33] Wesley stays in that vein. Hymn 124 sums up the way Wesley's spirituality is both imbued with imagery of sacrifice and careful that our offering does not repeat the offering of Christ. He interprets anamnesis, bringing memory to life, as a matter of experiencing *anew* the "once and for all" sacrifice:

>   Angels and Men might strive in vain,
>   They could not add the smallest Grain
>   T'augment thy Death's Atoning Power,
>   The Sacrifice is all-compleat,
>   The Death Thou never canst repeat,
>   Once offer'd up to die no more.
>
>   Yet may we celebrate below,
>   And daily thus thine Offering shew

29. Wesley and Wesley, *Lord's Supper*, 72.
30. Wesley and Wesley, *Lord's Supper*, 12.
31. Wesley and Wesley, *Lord's Supper*, 18.
32. Wesley and Wesley, *Lord's Supper*, 20.
33. Eslinger, *Holy Mystery*, 22.

> Expos'd before thy Father's Eyes;
> In this tremendous Mystery
> Present Thee bleeding on the Tree,
> Our everlasting Sacrifice . . .[34]

I realize this may be a lot for the reader to process, because there is so much use of this imagery of sacrifice in the Wesley brothers' Communion hymn lyrics. It is their preferred expression of this theme of anamnesis: doing this in remembrance of Christ. The Wesleys see our offering the meal as a way of bringing to fresh experience Christ's sacrificial offering.

A "Perpetual Sign"

While the Wesleys' use of offering imagery is largely limited to their hymn lyrics, the extent to which they placed importance on the frequency of the Lord's Supper is expressed in many other ways. In John Wesley's *Explanatory Notes*, he says regarding Mark 14:24: "That is, this I appoint to be a perpetual sign and memorial of my blood, as shed for establishing the New Covenant, that all who shall believe in me, may receive all its gracious promises."[35] Wesley considered it God's intention that Communion be practiced not only perpetually but quite often. In his sermon "The Duty of Constant Communion," which I quoted earlier, he said that the constant practice of Communion is important "because the benefits of doing it are so great to all that do it in obedience to him; namely, the forgiveness of our past sins and the present strengthening and refreshing of our souls." Wesley felt that Communion was a matter of "refreshing it [the soul] with the hope of glory."[36]

Wesley was in the habit of celebrating the Lord's Supper once every four days, and he "communicated with the same constancy at the age of 86 as he did at 36."[37] In encouraging people to practice

---

34. Wesley and Wesley, *Lord's Supper*, 105.
35. Wesley, *Explanatory Notes*, 158.
36. Outler and Heitzenrater, *John Wesley's Sermons*, 502.
37. Bowmer, *Sacrament*, 56.

Experiencing Anew

constant Communion, the Wesley brothers were, in part, addressing the emerging theme of "stillness" in Moravian teaching. The Moravians, whose profound early influence on Wesley will be visited in a later chapter, began to suffer from an "infection" of the doctrine of stillness at a society of Moravians Wesley frequently visited. They began to teach that without true faith, one ought to simply be *still* and abstain from the Lord's Supper and other practices. Ultimately, it was a point of contention that caused Wesley and others to withdraw from the society.[38]

For Wesley, the anamnesis of the table was vitally important! Remembrance was frequently experiencing and reexperiencing the presence of Christ. One hymn verse summarizes how anamnesis, for Wesley, connects us with the mystery of presence discussed earlier:

> We need not now go up to Heaven
>   To bring the long-sought Saviour down,
> Thou art to All already given:
>   Thou dost ev'n Now thy Banquet crown,
> To every faithful Soul appear,
> And shew thy Real Presence here.[39]

Wesley saw anamnesis as bringing the sacrifice of Christ into present experience. This is not a matter of "imagining" that Jesus is here. On the contrary, Morrill says remembrance is letting God reimagine *us*, for God remembers who we really are, not just who we think we are. In that sense, it is "dangerous memory" that critiques our unthinking processes.[40] In anamnesis, God remembers us as we remember the topsy-turvy, upside-down values of the kingdom of God that we are called to. This is how our offering at this meal brings us into participation in the sacrifice of Christ, which was done once and for all but is brought into fresh awareness each and every time we gather around the table.

Dick Eslinger has made a case for the way in which the 1972 liturgy in the Service of Word and Table published by the United

---

38. Bowmer, *Sacrament*, 38–39.

39. Wesley and Wesley, *Lord's Supper*, 99.

40. Morrill elaborates on this idea throughout his book *Anamnesis as Dangerous Memory*.

Something Happens Here

Methodist Church used the words "experience anew" for anamnesis. This was repeated in a 1980 supplement. He argues, and rightly so, that these words were "attuned to Methodist liturgical piety," though they were dropped from the 1989 *United Methodist Hymnal* and 1992 *Book of Worship*.[41]

Remembrance is the first important set of colors that emerges from turning the prism and seeing how the "sure and real" presence of Christ takes expression. We *experience anew* Christ's self-giving love. His gift comes alive and is made fresh. After seeing Wesley's extensive use of the biblical image of sacrifice in hymns, I propose that the words "experience anew" should be brought back into the liturgy. In the meantime, when I place the broken bread in the hands of a hungry parishioner, I typically say, "Take, eat, and experience the presence of Christ" instead of "Remember that Christ died for you." I try to sprinkle preaching and teaching with this sense of anamnesis. Eslinger suggests this should be done "with the goal of deepening the worshipper's pilgrimage into the depth of the atonement and, more expansively, the mystery of the incarnation. Put simply, 'making anamnesis,' means that the saving acts of God being represented, or 'experienced anew,' will resonate with the congregation's immersion in the biblical narratives."[42]

This chapter has explored a fundamental feature of Wesleyan spirituality, trusting that Jesus knew what he was doing when calling us to experience and reexperience what we already know to be true. The presence of Christ is embodied in the gathered community instead of simply impressing itself upon our minds, because the Lord knows that we must grow into being who we are. This is the first of three bands of color that emerge when Wesley holds our imaginative Communion prism up to the beautiful light of Christ's presence. *Experiencing anew* the sacrifice of Christ is the theme of remembrance generally, but it is vividly found in the biblical images of Charles and John Wesleys' lyrics in particular.

---

41. Eslinger, *Holy Mystery*, 154.
42. Eslinger, *Holy Mystery*, 174.

Experiencing Anew

Invited to Participate in the Life of God

I love to "read" my copy of one of the most well-known icons from the Orthodox tradition of the Eastern Church, Rublov's icon "The Trinity." The original resides in a monastery at the base of Mount Sinai. It is sometimes called "The Hospitality of Abraham" because it depicts the three visitors who came to visit Abraham and Sarah in Gen 18 from the eyes of Trinitarian theology and spirituality. I notice that the figures of Christ and the Holy Spirit gently nod toward God the Father. I observe the colors the three figures wear, for they certainly have meaning. I recognize that they don't have particularly masculine or feminine features, and they each hold a scepter of sorts. They are all sitting at the table, with Christ's hand over the blessing cup.

The more time I spend reading this icon—partly because of its characteristic use of spatial detail—there is a sense in which I feel drawn into the picture. The body shapes of the three figures around the table form an embodied circle of sorts. The table is itself shaped like a chalice, and the vivid yellow-gold color makes that feature stand out, as if the table is a chalice being extended to me. Most of all, I notice that there is an extra place at the table, as if the icon is inviting me to pull up a chair. The icon is a vivid reminder that we are invited into the circle of grace, into real participation in the life of God. Communion is not a mental exercise but a fully embodied experience.

For me, that's the power of remembrance. This invitation into the life of God is becoming lost in a sea tainted with North American religiosity. I was watching a famous megachurch pastor on TV a few years ago, noticing the sculpture of a revolving world behind him (and the conspicuous lack of a cross in their worship space). He boldly said, "Jesus came to make all your dreams come true." I confess that I thought to myself, "No, that's Disney World . . . Jesus came to *save* us." This typified prosperity spirituality, one of the most unique American heresies, along with another dangerous unorthodox companion: fundamentalism. Our Christian calling is not to be rich or to be right but to be in *relationship* with God and one another.

Something Happens Here

It is most profound that Jesus said, "Do this in remembrance of *me*." He did not say to do this in remembrance of this ritual or these words, in remembrance of that moment in time, or in remembrance of the cross that all this represents. He said, "Do this in remembrance of *me*." That meant "Do this in remembrance of all of me . . . all my teaching, all my love, all my life, all of who I am." In our times of acute anxiety about our institutional brokenness, it appears to me that we tend to do Communion in remembrance of each other instead. We are thinking about who is invited and whether anyone is truly excluded, or working through the mental calisthenics of loving people without accepting them, or hyper-focusing on what disqualifies someone from being the celebrant. How odd that we would find pockets of the church splintering off over culture war issues rather than being united by the one who invites us all to do so in remembrance of him, not in remembrance of us.

Conspicuously, some of the things we get most divided over in contemporary religious life aren't even mentioned in the Gospels at all, nor are they addressed in the ancient creeds. There are various opinions on these matters among faithful Christians, but without Christ, religion so easily falls back into Pharisee religion. It's as if it is not enough to choose what seems right for your life, faithfully interpreting Scripture through tradition, reason, and experience. Religion can so easily become about making sure everybody else thinks and acts right. We simply don't like any challenges that threaten our worldview. But it's not about me. It's about God, and everything about God is in Christ, the exact imprint of God's very being.[43] We must abandon our worship of what I often call the "new trinity" (me, myself, and I).

Clearly, experiencing anew the sacrifice of Christ in the very offering of ourselves is part of the breadth of colors Wesley revealed and that we need to fathom once again. Next, we will consider a second band of color that emerges when we hold the Communion prism up to the light.

---

43. Heb 1:3.

4

Becoming All Flame

THE FIRST SEVERAL YEARS of ministry were both exciting and difficult. I had the incredible opportunity of starting a new church while my wife and I were raising our family, and it was an experience I will always treasure. However, there were bumps and bruises along the way, especially in the season when two staff and a small but vocal group of families abruptly left the new congregation, which had been meeting in a high school auditorium, and dispersed to a variety of churches with more Pentecostal approaches. For a time, I blamed myself, but I later realized how formative this faith experience was for both me and the congregation. I stayed six or seven more years, and this was one of those moments that truly forged us as a United Methodist Church.

In that period of my early thirties, I discovered that there is a mystic within me that has been crying out for my entire life. For a time, I had let that "dancer" within me free but provided her little structure, and she was "blown about by every wind of doctrine."[1] Then, for a time, I reacted to the pain of failure by stuffing the mystic back into the dark recesses of my soul and went back to the world of doing and functioning. I plummeted because I was, in

1. Eph 4:14.

effect, shutting off a part of myself. God has shown me that this has been the grand pendulum swing of my spiritual life throughout my journey, though it had not been this extreme before. It became clear to me that the "mystic in me" needed the nurture of spiritual formation studies to be truly free and yet grounded in faith.

This experience led to the gift of the tree, a scriptural image that has become my most sacred spiritual metaphor. During one of my private retreat visits to the community called Sacred Heart Monastery in Cullman, Alabama, after spending two days in arduous studies, internal struggles, and prayer, I became suddenly enthralled by an extremely large magnolia tree that rests near the front door of the property. I spent two hours contemplating under that tree, examining its large trunk, admiring its extensive branches and leaves. I was overwhelmed with the simple thought that in order for this tree to grow so large, firm, and beautiful—in order for this tree to reach up to God and reach out to the world in love—it must have something I could not see. It must have expansive roots. Roots were what I desperately needed.

I had spent too much of my life trying to expand my branches while ignoring my roots, and this led to a "top-heavy" spirituality over the years. I was doing more and more, yet I was not focused on what I was becoming. I had striven to reach out to God, make music that glorifies my Creator, and make a difference in the world. These are all good things, but I had not nourished the roots I so desperately needed. I had discovered the things of the Spirit but had neglected the things of the soul. To stay with the metaphor, it took an experience of "fallen-ness" to show this truth to me.

Since that day, grounding myself in exploration of the deepest of Christian spiritual traditions has helped me to strengthen my roots. I have found that when it comes to the things of the Spirit, structure is a very good thing. Surprising, I know. I long to "be like a tree planted by water, sending out its roots by the stream. It shall not fear when heat comes, and its leaves shall stay green; in the year of drought it is not anxious, and it does not cease to bear fruit."[2]

---

2. Jer 17:8.

I've since discovered that the sacred tree of the Scriptures,[3] growing tall and strong in order to stretch its branches up to God and out to the world in love, is not the only biblical metaphor that vividly describes what it means to become a more complete human being. Perhaps the Christian life is so mysterious that only metaphors will do. Allow me to introduce you to an ancient pioneer of spiritual formation, one who shaped John Wesley's theology very much and who explored an amazing set of biblical metaphors to discover what it means to be people who come to the table as those who are becoming more Christlike, finding our true self.

If the Wesleys held Communion up to the light as a prism, we have seen the shining mystery of the presence of Christ in the gathered community. The previous chapter identified the first important way colors emerge when holding up the lens with Wesley: that of *experiencing anew* the sacrifice of Christ in our present-day offering. For Wesley, this does not repeat Christ's sacrifice but brings it to *life*.

In this chapter, I hope to show how the experience of Christ's presence in our midst while sharing Communion is illuminated by turning the symbolic prism to reveal a second rainbow of colors: the vision that we are growing in sanctification, or what Wesley calls "Christian perfection." The best way to explore this is to introduce you to the biggest historical source of Wesley's theology of personal growth and development, Macarius.

Macarius the Egyptian

Macarius the Egyptian was a fourth-century desert monk. He is described as "unforgettable," one about whom "there is a great deal that is hard to believe."[4] One ancient historian adds, "They used to say that he was in an unending ecstasy and that he spent more time involved with God than with the things beneath heaven,"[5]

---

3. See Gen 2, Ps 1, Jer 17, and Rev 22.
4. Palladius of Aspuna, *Lausiac History*, 33.
5. Palladius of Aspuna, *Lausiac History*, 35.

Macarius was caught up in the bliss of prayer as well as the sanctification of the soul.

There is a widespread assumption in the academic world that John Wesley was heavily influenced by the fourth-century *Fifty Spiritual Homilies* attributed to Macarius. This is hard to refute, since Wesley included the *Homilies* in his fifty-volume *Christian Library* and quoted the *Homilies* near the beginning of his well-known sermon "The Scripture Way of Salvation":

> How exactly did Macarius, fourteen hundred years ago, describe the present experience of the children of God! "The unskillful" (or unexperienced), when grace operates, presently imagine they have no more sin. Whereas they that have discretion cannot deny, that even we who have the grace of God may be molested again . . . For we have often had instances of some among the brethren, who have experienced such grace as to affirm that they had no sin in them. And yet after all, when they thought themselves entirely freed from it, the corruption that lurked within was stirred up anew, and they were well-nigh burnt up.[6]

Wesley is referring to Macarius when discussing "sanctifying grace," which Wesley sees as grace that deepens the process of inner renewal, starting with the experience of justification by faith. Wesley notes that though temptations return, we have entered the gradual work of becoming more dead to sin and alive to God. "The Scripture Way of Salvation" is essential reading for Wesley's teaching on sanctification and Christian perfection.

Scholars assume to varying degrees how much Wesley was directly influenced by the author of the *Homilies*,[7] but it's clear this fourth-century monk had a great deal of impact on him. In this chapter, I invite you to immerse yourself with me in the Macarian *Homilies* and discover the concept of sanctification through

6. Outler and Heitzenrater, *John Wesley's Sermons*, 374.

7. See Snyder, "Macarius the Egyptian," 55–56. He notes that scholars debate the extent that this Eastern ideal of "perfection" was unique to Macarius or a reflection of his dependence on Gregory of Nyssa (c. 330–95), which Wesley also read because of his fascination with Eastern thought.

Becoming All Flame

divinization, or *theosis*, found there. We will be able to identify threads of Macarian spirituality woven into Wesley's theology of sanctification and see how he connects our journey toward Christian perfection with the power and effect of Christ's presence at the table.

The Macarian *Homilies* read as passionate sermons, and it is not difficult to see why they have been read by people such as Wesley interested in the progress of the soul toward holiness. They feature the imagination and allegorical reading of Scripture typical of Alexandrian spirituality of his time, with lots of references to theosis, the Eastern concept of becoming like God, or entering into union with God. I believe there are five important motifs threaded into various homilies in the collection, and these will help us discover what is distinctive about the vision of sanctification found in the *Fifty Spiritual Homilies* and the spirituality adopted by Wesley.

First, the *Homilies* feature a motif of the soul as chariot, palace, or ship of God. For him, the soul is the place God dwells. With the prophet Ezekiel's vision of the chariot, the first homily presents the scriptural story as a prototype for divinization, or becoming like God: "And all of this which the prophet saw in ecstasy or in a trance was indeed true and certain, but it was only signifying and foreshadowing something no less hidden, something divine and mysterious . . . For the prophet was viewing the mystery of the human soul that would receive its Lord and would become his throne of glory."[8] It is a moving throne, taking the soul somewhere. Christ, "the good and useful and the only authentic Charioteer,"[9] is one who "guides it with the reins of the Spirit."[10] Again, "where God himself truly mounts and guides the soul," God is "skillfully directing and leading with expertise the chariot of the soul."[11]

Just as the soul is a throne or chariot for Christ, he also says Christ takes dwelling in the "palace" of the soul. In the fifteenth homily, in a discussion that resembles the later writings of Teresa

---

8. Pseudo-Macarius, *Fifty Spiritual Homilies*, 37.
9. Pseudo-Macarius, *Fifty Spiritual Homilies*, 39.
10. Pseudo-Macarius, *Fifty Spiritual Homilies*, 38.
11. Pseudo-Macarius, *Fifty Spiritual Homilies*, 42.

of Ávila, Macarius writes that there are "infinite depths to the human heart. There are found reception rooms, bedrooms, doors and ante-chambers, many offices and exits . . . the heart is the palace of Christ."[12] Macarius notes that "all creation is ruled by him, and still he did not establish his throne in them . . . But it was only with man that he was pleased, fellowshipping and resting in him."[13]

Finally, in the forty-fourth homily, he uses the metaphor of the ship: "No one can by himself pass over and cross the sea unless he has a light and buoyant boat made of wood . . . in a similar way, no person of himself can cross and pass over the bitter sea of sin and the dangerous abyss of the evil powers of the darkness of the passions, unless he receive the buoyant and heavenly and winged Spirit of Christ." He adds imagery for how the soul is nourished: "As those on the boat do not draw up water from the sea and drink it nor have their clothing from the sea nor their food, but they carry these things aboard the ship from land, so too Christians do not receive from this world, but from above, from Heaven, heavenly food and spiritual raiment." He follows with the reminder that every ship needs a pilot, and ours is Christ himself.[14] In the Macarian *Homilies*, these images of divine indwelling de-emphasize our efforts in growing toward likeness or union with God and emphasize the role of divine presence within. *Theosis* is a process of divine entry into our lives, or "enthronement," and relinquishing control to the one who best holds the reigns.

Second, the *Homilies* feature a motif of light, fire, and the irradiation of the soul. Homily 47 begins with Moses' face being difficult for the people to bear: "So now Christians receive that glory of light in their souls, and the darkness, not bearing the splendor of the light, is blinded and is put to flight."[15] God's people have "the Lord Himself shining in their hearts."[16] The apostles model this, because they were "lights to their own proper house of

---

12. Pseudo-Macarius, *Fifty Spiritual Homilies*, 120.
13. Pseudo-Macarius, *Fifty Spiritual Homilies*, 229.
14. Pseudo-Macarius, *Fifty Spiritual Homilies*, 225.
15. Pseudo-Macarius, *Fifty Spiritual Homilies*, 132.
16. Pseudo-Macarius, *Fifty Spiritual Homilies*, 141.

Israel. The Apostles were also suns, sending off rays in every part of the whole world."[17]

Let's return to the vision of Ezekiel's chariot in the first homily to see this theme. The writer discusses the four creatures and their incomprehensible number of eyes, noting that an enlightened soul is "completely illuminated with the unspeakable beauty of the glory of the light of the face of Christ" and "becomes all light, all face, all eye."[18] He returns to this in Homily 32, noting that Ezekiel "presents them to us as eyes all over. In a similar way also is the soul that carries God, or rather that is carried by God—it becomes all eye."[19]

A unique feature of the image of light is its connection with the resurrection of the body. Christ "now mystically illumines the soul," and this light is somewhat hidden "until the day of resurrection, when even the body itself will reign with the soul . . . and is illuminated by the divine life."[20] Easter is the prototype for our own resurrection, which will complete what is only partial: "The glory of the Holy Spirit rises up from within, covering and warming the bodies of the saints . . . their bodies shall be glorified by means of the light which even now is in them hiddenly."[21] The writer uses the metaphor of fire as well as light. In the day of resurrection, "that same fire which now interiorly directs their hearts, bursts forth upon the dissolution of the body." For now, "faithful souls receive in an interior way that divine and heavenly fire in this present life, and that fire fashions a heavenly image upon their human nature." This image will be "manifested exteriorly in the resurrection."[22]

Finally, Homily 43 begins with yet another metaphor, Christian community around one holy fire: "As many lights and burning lamps are lighted from fire, but the lamps and lights are lighted and

---

17. Pseudo-Macarius, *Fifty Spiritual Homilies*, 107.
18. Pseudo-Macarius, *Fifty Spiritual Homilies*, 37–38.
19. Pseudo-Macarius, *Fifty Spiritual Homilies*, 202.
20. Pseudo-Macarius, *Fifty Spiritual Homilies*, 46–47.
21. Pseudo-Macarius, *Fifty Spiritual Homilies*, 73.
22. Pseudo-Macarius, *Fifty Spiritual Homilies*, 91.

Something Happens Here

shine from one nature, so also Christians are enkindled and shine from one nature, the divine fire, the Son of God, and they have their lamps burning in their hearts." The fire both enlightens the soul and burns away evil: "As sticks are thrown into the fire and are unable to resist the power of the fire, but are burned up at once, so too demons, seeking to wage war against a man who has received the Spirit, are burned and consumed by the divine power of the fire ... they are burned up by prayer, like wax by fire."[23] This leads to a third observation.

Third, the *Homilies* feature a motif of spiritual progression through struggle. The sense that wrestling with evil is part of the spiritual life is squarely in keeping with the fathers and mothers of the desert. What is distinctive in the *Homilies*, however, is the idea that the fight commences after one "tastes the grace of God," for this is how God tests us once we turn toward heaven.[24] God begins a divine moderation, holding back on the outpouring of grace so we experience no more than is needed. In discussing Moses in the forty-seventh homily, the writer sees the escape from Egypt as a paradigm: "But the spiritual Pharaoh, the king of darkness of sin, when it knows that the soul is in revolt and is fleeing out of his kingdom," chases after us. When God sees that the soul is terrorized, God "helps and deals patiently with the soul and tests it." God dispensed the grace of making a way through the Red Sea.[25] Likewise, Christianity is "tasting deeply of truth," and then God pulls back and "withdraws and allows the man to be tested and afflicted." God does this "that you may become humble and all the more eagerly seek him." It is not that grace is weak—rather, in order that free will may be tested, grace "permits the presence of sin."[26]

The writer envisions two "battles," two conflicts we must endure—one in the "material affairs" of this life and the other "in the interior." As we move through struggle, each of us is "able to find in

---

23. Pseudo-Macarius, *Fifty Spiritual Homilies*, 219–20.
24. Pseudo-Macarius, *Fifty Spiritual Homilies*, 115.
25. Pseudo-Macarius, *Fifty Spiritual Homilies*, 236–37.
26. Pseudo-Macarius, *Fifty Spiritual Homilies*, 177.

Becoming All Flame

his heart another struggle, another hidden opposition, and another war of the temptations of the evil spirits, and another battle opens up."[27] Some never realize there is a wrestling within, because they are engrossed in the struggles on the outside. Christians "ought to prepare themselves for the struggle and battle . . . afflictions, both exterior and those interior wars, so that, when struck, they may rise to higher victories through endurance."[28] The difference between true Christians and others is not outward appearance but in the renewing of the mind: "Christians possess a glory and beauty and an indescribable heavenly richness that come to them with hard work and sweat, acquired in times of temptation and many trials, and many conflicts. All of this must be ascribed to God's grace."[29]

There is no advice given about how to fight these demons, yet he claims that "to uproot sin and the evil that is so imbedded in our sinning can be done only by divine power . . . To struggle, yes, to continue to fight, to inflict blows, and to receive setbacks is in your power. To uproot, however, belongs to God alone."[30] His remedy is to participate in what God is doing through prayer: "So also the soul should be totally concentrated on asking and on a loving movement toward the Lord, not wandering and dispersed by its thoughts." This is how a person is "enflamed with divine passion and fiery desire from a spiritual love toward God and . . . receives the grace of the sanctifying perfection of the Spirit."[31] He likens us to a "bronze vessel" you put burning fuel under so that the insides are made warm: "So also grace, the heavenly fire, is also within you. Hence if you pray and give your thoughts to the love of Christ, see how you have thrown under yourself the wood and your thoughts become fire and are immersed completely in the desire for God."[32]

---

27. Pseudo-Macarius, *Fifty Spiritual Homilies*, 154.
28. Pseudo-Macarius, *Fifty Spiritual Homilies*, 112.
29. Pseudo-Macarius, *Fifty Spiritual Homilies*, 65.
30. Pseudo-Macarius, *Fifty Spiritual Homilies*, 48.
31. Pseudo-Macarius, *Fifty Spiritual Homilies*, 214.
32. Pseudo-Macarius, *Fifty Spiritual Homilies*, 216.

Fourth, the *Homilies* feature a motif of the mingling of grace and free will. In the forty-first homily, the soul is described as deep soil. Like the roots of a tree, sin and grace can both reach deeply into the soul. God overcomes this partially: "If, therefore, the working of divine grace overshadows the soul according to the degree of each person's faith and he receives help from above, grace still overshadows him only in a certain degree." Our task is to "lend" ourselves completely to grace, so that grace "sinks roots even to the deepest levels."[33] The image of roots frames the writer's understanding of the mingling of free will and grace. He says, "If, then, anyone loves God, God also shares his love with him. Once a person believes in him, God bestows on such a one a heavenly faith . . . As you offer God any part of yourself, he himself shares with your soul similar aspects of his own being."[34]

This motif is found in the very first homily. The writer notes that by allowing Christ to hold the reigns as our Charioteer, "our bodies will be judged worthy of his honor at the resurrection which even now the human soul is given an anticipated grasp of such a glory by being mingled with the Spirit."[35] Homily 9 begins with God's gracious initiative to mingle with our effort: "The spiritual power of God's grace, working within the soul, does so with the greatest patience, wisdom, and mystical touching of the mind. The individual also struggles in great patience in the opportunities that come his way. But then the work of grace works perfectly in him. This is seen in the fact that his free will, after great temptation, is clearly bent on pleasing the Holy Spirit."[36] He surveys biblical characters, noting that grace "comes forth with much contention" and tests free will.[37] This calls us to cleave to God with singular purpose. Macarius believes "it does this so that, by such battling, longing, and diligent seeking, the mind may be rendered worthy

---

33. Pseudo-Macarius, *Fifty Spiritual Homilies*, 217.
34. Pseudo-Macarius, *Fifty Spiritual Homilies*, 116.
35. Pseudo-Macarius, *Fifty Spiritual Homilies*, 39.
36. Pseudo-Macarius, *Fifty Spiritual Homilies*, 83–84.
37. Pseudo-Macarius, *Fifty Spiritual Homilies*, 85.

Becoming All Flame

... of the gift and grace of Christ, resting in the vessel of the soul."[38] This mingling is illustrated beautifully with Martha and Mary. The writer notes that when Mary loved Jesus, "he endowed her with certain hidden power from his very own being . . . But not long after, the works of service, that Martha kindly performed, brought her also to that gift of grace."[39] To Macarius, they were simply at different places on their journeys of mingling with grace.

Practical images of leaven and kneading illuminate his thoughts about the mingling of grace and human effort: "Take for example a person kneading flour without putting into it a leaven. However much be the efforts he makes, turning it over and over and thoroughly working it up, still the lump remains unleavened and unfit to eat. But if leaven is put into the dough, it draws to itself the whole mass of dough."[40] We are mistaken when we rely on our own strength, for the leaven of grace affects everything. The idea in the *Homilies* is that Christ's grace persuades, yet we have to respond to God's invitation to knead the yeast into the dough of life. If we lose favor with God, "it is not that God is changeable or of a foolish mind . . . but the fact is that human beings themselves do not consent to grace and on account of this they go astray."[41]

I believe Macarius was ahead of his time on the theological problem of grace and free will. God's grace acts with various "refreshings," just as we respond in different ways. He observes, "So varied are the ways that grace affects such persons and leads the soul in so many different paths, refreshing it in accord with the will of God. Grace exercises the soul differently in order to restore it to the heavenly Father perfect and faultless and pure."[42] At times, grace holds back, but Christ overcomes. Thinking imaginatively of Christ as a gardener with the cross as his tool, Macarius writes, "The heavenly and true cultivator, when he came to humanity made barren by evil, put on the body and carried the cross as his

---

38. Pseudo-Macarius, *Fifty Spiritual Homilies*, 87.
39. Pseudo-Macarius, *Fifty Spiritual Homilies*, 103–4.
40. Pseudo-Macarius, *Fifty Spiritual Homilies*, 158.
41. Pseudo-Macarius, *Fifty Spiritual Homilies*, 122.
42. Pseudo-Macarius, *Fifty Spiritual Homilies*, 145.

tool and worked the barren soul and removed it from the thorns and thistles of evil spirits and pulled the weeds of sin and burned up with fire every weed of its sins. And in this way he cultivated it with the wood of the cross."[43]

This is mingling with God's grace, because we participate by giving our assent: "Just as the portrait painter is attentive to the face of the king as he paints, and, when the face of the king is directly opposite . . . he paints the portrait easily and well," Macarius writes, "in a similar way the good portrait painter, Christ, for those who believe him and gaze continually toward him, at once paints according to his own image a heavenly man." Christ is the artist, but ours is the attentiveness: "It is necessary that we gaze on him, believing and loving him, casting aside all else and attending to him so that he may paint his own heavenly image and send it into our souls."[44]

Fifth, the *Homilies* feature a motif of degrees of perfection in the spiritual life. Elaborating on the previously discussed motif of fire and light, the thirty-sixth homily begins: "The resurrection of the souls of the dead takes place even now in the time of death. But the resurrection of bodies will take place in that day. Just as in the heavens the stars are fixed, but all are not equal, one differing from the other (1 Corinthians 15:41) in brightness and magnitude, so also in spiritual matters there are degrees of progress, according 'to the measure of faith.'"[45]

While all souls are not equal in brightness, we are all on a journey of being changed by grace: "Like a bee that secretly fashions its comb in the hive, so also grace secretly forms in hearts its own love. It changes to sweetness what is bitter, what is rough into what is smooth."[46] With these words in the sixteenth homily, the writer gives us a striking image of the change of the heart over time. Humanity is "divinized," or made more holy, by the grace of God. We may struggle with the rough edges of our personality, but in

43. Pseudo-Macarius, *Fifty Spiritual Homilies*, 185.
44. Pseudo-Macarius, *Fifty Spiritual Homilies*, 191.
45. Pseudo-Macarius, *Fifty Spiritual Homilies*, 206.
46. Pseudo-Macarius, *Fifty Spiritual Homilies*, 132.

Becoming All Flame

time, the heart is reformed from bitter to sweet. Perhaps this vivid image of the bee best summarizes Macarias's view of sanctification, though other metaphors are used as well: "Take the example of the undeveloped infant in the womb. It does not immediately grow into a matured person but only gradually it receives the shape and is born, and even then is not perfect, but it grows gradually over many years," and just as seeds do not take root the moment they are put in the ground, and the person who plants a pear tree does not at once eat its fruit, "so likewise also in spiritual things."[47]

Striving is our purpose in this image of growing toward spiritual perfection: "You see how many stages and ways of the Spirit's acting there are. Evil is cut out little by little and diminished, not all at once."[48] His advice is to strive continually, but never pass judgment on anyone else. We look on others as if they are whole, with compassion and tenderheartedness. We realize that very few reach true perfection—very few "have love for God alone" and are "detached from all others."[49] Hence it is a matter of degrees, or measures: "There is a struggle, a conflict, a discernment between what is of the love of God and what is of the love of the world."[50] Macarius continues, "But because of this there lie along the path temptations and many trials and afflictions and struggles and sweat in order to sift out those who have truly loved the Lord . . . and have desired nothing else along with their love for him."[51] In short, the perspective of the *Homilies* is that we are being molded into the image of Christ, to some degree, as we proceed on life's journey toward wholeness. "If, therefore, you have become a throne of God and the Heavenly Charioteer has mounted you and your whole soul is a spiritual eye and has become totally light . . . if finally your interior man has experienced all these and has been rooted in the

---

47. Pseudo-Macarius, *Fifty Spiritual Homilies*, 124.
48. Pseudo-Macarius, *Fifty Spiritual Homilies*, 111.
49. Pseudo-Macarius, *Fifty Spiritual Homilies*, 66.
50. Pseudo-Macarius, *Fifty Spiritual Homilies*, 67.
51. Pseudo-Macarius, *Fifty Spiritual Homilies*, 71.

abundance of faith, then, behold, you already live the eternal life, indeed, with your soul resting with the Lord."[52]

In the *Homilies*, this is not a matter of ever-climbing a spiritual ladder. We strive for it, but the measure of perfection waxes and wanes: "There are times when grace burns more brightly, consoles and refurbishes more completely. Then at other times the grace subsides and is clouded over."[53] The writer boldly states that he has never seen a perfect Christian, for sin is always present though it is under grace's influence. When asked what measure of grace he, Macarius, is in, he notes that though he had been given an ecstatic experience of the sign of the cross imprinting itself in light upon him, he still regards others with "pure eyes" and rejoices with their journey. There is no sense of arrival. God simply opens the door to more progression: "From a hundred mansions he enters into another hundred."[54]

The seventeenth homily begins with these words: "Perfect Christians, who are considered worthy to reach a degree of perfection and to come close to the King, are continually dedicated to the cross of Christ."[55] He illustrates that the friend of an emperor should not be surprised to be shown the secrets of a palace. Christians should likewise not be surprised to learn the secrets of grace: "But then grace comes, and completely removes the veil."[56] Some souls "obtain fully the illumination and participation with fullness of grace of the hidden and mystical Communion with the Holy Spirit." Others are deceived:

> Such ones as these, having received the grace of the Spirit, enjoy the consolation of grace in peace and longing and spiritual sweetness. But they begin to rely on this fact and become puffed up. They live securely and forget the need for a broken heart and humility of spirit. They cease stretching out to attain the perfect measure of emptiness

---

52. Pseudo-Macarius, *Fifty Spiritual Homilies*, 44.
53. Pseudo-Macarius, *Fifty Spiritual Homilies*, 82.
54. Pseudo-Macarius, *Fifty Spiritual Homilies*, 83.
55. Pseudo-Macarius, *Fifty Spiritual Homilies*, 135.
56. Pseudo-Macarius, *Fifty Spiritual Homilies*, 136.

Becoming All Flame

from passions. They fail to be filled with grace in all diligence and faith. But they felt secured and became complacent with their scanty consolations of grace.[57]

So, his pastoral advice is to "go to the shore of the river and drink as much as you need and continue on your way, not worrying about the river's source or how it flows," just as we see the light of the sun but don't ask how much light is in it, and as a babe comes to the breast but doesn't search for the wellspring from which the milk flows. There is no real arrival at perfection, except perfection in love: "If one has reached this degree, he has arrived at the perfect love of Christ and the fullness of the Godhead."[58]

These five motifs observed in the *Fifty Spiritual Homilies*—the image of Christ riding in the chariot of the soul, the image of divine light and fire in us, the image of our wrestling against sin and evil, the image of the mingling of grace and free will, and the image of measures of perfection in the spiritual life—paint a unique picture of theosis, or divinization. It is characteristic of fourth-century desert spirituality, but at the same time, aspects of it are distinct to the Macarian tradition. It is no wonder Wesley read this work with great interest.

The Influence of Macarius on Wesley

The influence of the Macarian *Homilies* is obvious in Wesley's work. Though Wesley was not a systematic but a practical theologian, it is easy to see that his core teachings on the "way of salvation" are threaded with concepts from the *Homilies*. The first thing to note is that for both writers, we experience sanctification in this life that comes from God's initiative. Wesley's Arminian approach is more than a critique of the Calvinist view of predestination; it is an exacting and careful theological resolution of the problem of the mingling of grace and free will. The way of salvation is, for Wesley, entirely a matter of grace. Specifically, this involves three

---

57. Pseudo-Macarius, *Fifty Spiritual Homilies*, 89.
58. Pseudo-Macarius, *Fifty Spiritual Homilies*, 110.

Something Happens Here

movements of grace—prevenient grace (which initiates, woos, and moves before our awareness or response), justifying grace (which restores our broken relationship with God, experienced when we turn our hearts to the divine), and sanctifying grace (which takes us on a journey toward holiness, making us more like Christ, "from one degree of glory to another"[59]). In reading the *Homilies*, one gets the sense that Wesley adopted the Macarian view of the mingling between grace and human effort, yet Wesley read it through post-Reformation glasses and articulated it with careful post-Reformation language to avoid any sense of works righteousness.[60] It is all ascribed to grace.

Second, with the Macarian tradition, Wesley believed that sanctification is something that can be partially experienced on earth in what Wesley described as moving toward "Christian perfection."[61] "What is it to be sanctified?" Wesley asked. "To be renewed in the image of God."[62] Bouteneff says it well: "The Wesleyan conviction that salvation was a matter of *this* world found reflection in an acute sense that perfection was not only to be striven for in this world, but also was attainable." He adds that at the same time, Wesley "provides qualifying statements about what is not yet possible in this world, to the point of saying that there is no absolute perfection on earth, nor indeed has Wesley ever met a person who has attained all the marks of sanctification, and believes there can in fact be none such in the world."[63]

---

59. 2 Cor 3:18.

60. It is beyond the scope of this book to elaborate on Wesley's teachings on prevenient, justifying, and sanctifying grace. He discusses it at length in the sermon referenced above, "The Scripture Way of Salvation," found in Outler and Heitzenrater, *John Wesley's Sermons*, 371–80.

61. Outler and Heitzenrater, *John Wesley's Sermons*, 69–84.

62. John Wesley, "A Plain Account of Christian Perfection," qtd. in Whaling, *John and Charles Wesley*, 319.

63. Peter C. Bouteneff, "All Creation in United Thanksgiving: Gregory of Nyssa and the Wesleys on Salvation," in Kimbrough, *Orthodox and Wesleyan Spirituality*, 196. Here, Bouteneff discusses the influence of the Macarian *Homilies* on Wesley's "practical theology," though he takes the position that the Wesleys did not read much of Gregory of Nyssa, who shares a similar concept of perfection.

Becoming All Flame

It could be said that the song of both great preachers is "By grace we strive, though we never arrive." Both saw struggle and effort as essential elements in experiencing sanctification, though it comes entirely by grace. It is nothing more and nothing less than perfection in love, which can only be experienced by some measure, and never to its fullness in this life. Yes, Wesley's writings and sermons are void of the vivid metaphors and scriptural allegories of the *Homilies* and are full of much more precise (and arguably dryer) language. But both speak with a common passion for perfection in love as the goal of Christianity.

This chapter has sought to illuminate the Wesleyan view of personal sanctification by exploring an ancient Eastern writer who influenced him greatly, identifying threads woven into Wesley's unique theology of Christian perfection. Now we will turn to evidence of these themes in Wesley's eucharistic teaching. One of his most explicit teachings on the sacrament is in his sermon "The Means of Grace," where he said, "All who desire an increase of the grace of God are to wait for it in partaking of the Lord's Supper."[64] This assumes a Macarian view of grace dispensed in measures. We will examine this sermon more carefully later, but in a sermon discussed earlier, "The Duty of Constant Communion," Wesley notes the value of coming to the table often, "like the first Christians, with whom the Christian sacrifice was a constant part of the Lord's Day service. And for several centuries they received it almost every day," to the point that they excommunicated those who refused to partake in this "continual remembrance."[65] For Wesley, "constant" Communion is a necessary ingredient in our ongoing, personal sanctification. One Wesley hymn sings, "And lo! my LORD is here become / The Bread of Life to *me*."[66] Another sings:

> Receive us then, Thou Pard'ning GOD,
> Partakers of his Flesh and Blood
>   Grant that we now may be:
> The Sp'rit's Attesting Seal impart,

---

64. Outler and Heitzenrater, *John Wesley's Sermons*, 165.
65. Outler and Heitzenrater, *John Wesley's Sermons*, 503.
66. Wesley and Wesley, *Lord's Supper*, 3, emphasis added.

And speak to every Sinner's Heart,
The Saviour died for Thee![67]

Wesley clearly believed that a personal encounter with Christ, the divine Word which God speaks to every heart, is experienced at the table. This encounter changes and forms us over time as we come again and again. Another eucharistic hymn sings of the awakening of our soul on its journey toward sanctification:

> And shall not We his Death partake,
>   In sympathetic Anguish groan?
> O Saviour, let thy Passion shake
>   Our Earth, and rent our Hearts of Stone,
> To second Life our Souls restore,
> And wake us that we sleep no more.[68]

The implications of this verse cannot be underestimated. For the Wesley brothers, the Lord's Supper brings to life the passion of Christ in a way that is both earth shaking and heart softening! It restores and awakens us to "second life," the life of sanctification. Yet another hymn specifies that this sanctification through the gift of the sacred meal is about moving us to perfection in love. It begins by singing of the "mingled stream" of blood and water, a notable reference to one of the Nonjuror usages discussed in a previous chapter. The last stanza sings of perfect love received in our hearts and practiced in our lives:

> The double Stream in Pardons rolls,
> And brings thy Love into our Souls,
> Who dare the Truth Divine receive,
> And Credence to thy Witness give,
> We here thy utmost Power shall prove
> Thy utmost Power of perfect Love.[69]

One of the most famous Wesley hymns, while not referring to the Eucharist or included in their collection of eucharistic hymns, sings most vividly of sanctification and invites God to "finish then

---

67. Wesley and Wesley, *Lord's Supper*, 9.
68. Wesley and Wesley, *Lord's Supper*, 20.
69. Wesley and Wesley, *Lord's Supper*, 24–25.

thy new creation" and change us "from glory into glory, / 'til in heaven we take our place."⁷⁰ Similarly, the thirtieth hymn in the eucharistic collection sings:

> The Cup of Blessing blest by Thee,
>   Let it thy Blood impart;
> The Bread thy Mystic Body be,
>   And cheer each languid Heart.
>
> The Grace which sure Salvation brings,
>   Let us herewith receive;
> Satiate the Hungry with good Things,
>   The Hidden Manna give.
>
> The Living Bread sent down from Heaven
>   In us vouchsafe to be:
> Thy Flesh for All the World is given,
>   And All may live by Thee.
>
> Now, LORD, on Us Thy Flesh bestow,
>   And let us drink Thy Blood,
> Till all our Souls are fill'd below
>   With all the Life of GOD.⁷¹

Here, the Wesleys sing of the "mystic body" given for all the world, that all may live by Christ. They see the "virtue, power, and effect" of Christ's presence as a matter of our ongoing sanctification, so that our souls are filled below with *all* the life of God. It is here that Wesley's view of sanctification is a natural complement to his sense of the real presence of Christ in the eucharistic assembly. This presence nourishes the Christian life through "constant" Communion, a spiritual practice which shapes and forms us through all the struggles life brings. Encountering Christ at the table continually draws us into union with God and moves us toward perfection in love. This spiritual formation is truly a "mingling" of the divine

---

70. Charles Wesley, "Love Divine, All Loves Excelling," in The United Methodist Church, *United Methodist Hymnal*, no. 384.

71. Wesley and Wesley, *Lord's Supper*, 24.

initiative of God's grace and the free will of the person who keeps coming back to the table to dine with Christ.

The Open Table and the Journey of Being Perfected in Love

I would imagine that even the least theologically educated United Methodist is likely to express a love for the open table. You don't have to be an adult. You don't have to be a member of that church—or any church, for that matter. The invitation is for all who hunger for God and seek to live a new life. Children are taught to come with open hands and open hearts to experience the love of Jesus. John Wesley called Communion a "converting ordinance," meaning that it changes us when we follow along with others in the faith.[72] It is one of the ways grace reaches out to us to grab hold of us over time.

I can remember when it dawned on me as a young man, at one of the closing Communion services at Sumatanga, the summer camp that I discussed earlier, that Christ gave himself for *me* . . . not just for the world in general. That was the first wave of grace that poured over me that day. The second was the realization that *all* my life, I had been invited to that table. I had always been most welcome there. The love of God has no beginning and no end.

Sometimes, I hear parents that come from other faith traditions decide not to bring their child to Communion because they don't understand it yet. Sometimes, I am brave enough to respond, "Yes, but they *do* understand being left out." So does the world right now as they observe our divisiveness over matters of human sexuality. I'm grateful that the grace imparted by Communion is not limited by my comprehension. What it does is form us over time, sometimes over a long period of time, into people of faith and love. There is a mingling of grace and free will always going on. The reason we have an open table is because we believe that love is flowing to us and growing in us, wherever we are. We are

---

72. Bowmer, *Sacrament*, 106–8.

all somewhere on the road, and we affirm wherever each of us are on the journey.

Is it truly an open table if some people are fully accepted and others are merely tolerated there? I think not. Love is growing toward perfection in all of us as we gather with the very people we have the most trouble loving. This is why, for the people of Corinth, Paul saw that the table was not just about "me and Jesus." At the table, love is revealed. God uncovers all of who God is, and God encounters all of who we are. The Communion table graces and refines; it shapes and renews. We come because we are always needing to grow in our love for God and each other.

Commitment to Christ is not just a ticket to heaven but the beginning of a journey of becoming more like Christ in light of the love poured out at the table. Coming to the table is a holy habit not because it always feels like a spectacular experience (only our cultural assumptions would assume it should) but because it shapes and forms us over time in ways we might not be fully aware of. We are baptized once, but we come to the table again and again. We are born once, but we need to eat and drink every day. We are justified by grace through faith, but we are always mingling with the love of God that pours out to us in endless measures.

I once served a local congregation in which a story was still circulating about one of my predecessors, who had threatened to stand at the door and refuse to let one of the relatives of a church family enter the building because they were different. This is unimaginable to me. Like the days of the early Christians in Corinth, we are prone to draw distinctions that God doesn't see and that Scripture does not make. When we discover differences we find difficult to navigate, perhaps we are being called to speak the truth in love and work toward reconciliation, yes. But we must do so with the understanding that everybody at the table is on the journey somewhere, and we must trust that grace is meeting them wherever they are.

There is no distinction at the table between saint and sinner, for all of us are a bit of both. The reason we practice an open table is not because we think nothing happens here but precisely because we believe all sorts of things happen here. God's grace pours out in "measures"—or, shall we say, in immeasurable ways for every person. In keeping with 1 Corinthians, what God *does* call each of us to do at the table is to honor the work of God in each other. If someone else at the table bothers you, I am fairly certain God is calling you to grow to love them with a love beyond your natural ability. God is calling you to become "all flame" and to love as God loves, and only God's glowing light can irradiate your soul in a way that forges the strength to do so.

5

Foretaste of Heaven

My mother, Betty Hamby West, died on the Sunday after Easter. She was the daughter, the niece, the wife, the sister, the mother, and the mother-in-law of Methodist preachers (some things can indeed run in the family). Mom had been faithful in her retirement from teaching English to attend the church where I served as founding pastor, and we had just entered our first building on the new property. As she had for fifty years, she taught Sunday school and started a new class.

Mom had a way of teaching me about life even in death. A few months before she died, we were still worshiping in the local high school auditorium one Sunday during Advent. She stood up when I opened the floor for prayer concerns. She said, "I have been diagnosed with a very aggressive form of cancer, and the prognosis is not good. But today, I want everybody to know that nothing is going to take the joy of my Christmas away!" She simply sat down, and that stunning moment was thereafter etched in my memory.

Just a few weeks after that, our congregation entered a brand-new sanctuary. She asked me to hold a service of anointing with prayers for healing there. I told her that I would be honored, and that I would do so on one condition—that she tell me what she believed about healing. I went to see her, and she told me all her thoughts about the difference between healing and curing, how there are many forms of healing (emotional, physical, spiritual, etc.), and that she believed the greatest healing is to fall into the arms of Jesus. She told me that she wanted to pray for whatever healing God had in store for her. Later, she and I truly believed she received an emotional healing from the experience.

After she died, the next Sunday was a Communion Sunday, and I dutifully served the people of my church. After serving the bread and the cup, I turned back toward the table to walk up the steps. I saw something. You may call it a vision or simply assume it was my imagination. But very clearly, in my mind's eye, I saw for a moment a vast choir seated around the Communion table. In a flash, I saw my mother there, smiling at me in the cloud of witnesses. It was an emotional moment that was difficult to process. I almost dropped the chalice.

I later thought of the famous words of Fanny Crosby's hymn "Blessed Assurance," truly an anthem of Methodist spirituality. The song sings, "Oh, what a foretaste of glory divine."[1] I had tasted of one that day indeed.

So far, we have discussed some of what is most distinctive about Wesley's Communion theology. We have looked at the mysterious effect of Christ's presence in the gathered community and the way Wesley seems to hold Communion up as a prism that shines the light of Christ's presence into distinct spectrums of color. The first assortment of colors discussed so far is related to remembrance (anamnesis), seen by Wesley through biblical images of Christ's sacrifice experienced anew in the offering of ourselves. The second is related to an Eastern view of personal sanctification (theosis), nourished by the "constant" practice of Communion as we move toward perfection in love.

By now, you have probably noticed that there is a method in our madness (or, should I say, a method in our Methodism). Each chapter identifies original sources of each distinct feature of Wesley's

---

1. Fanny Crosby, "Blessed Assurance," in The United Methodist Church, *United Methodist Hymnal*, no. 369.

Foretaste of Heaven

theology, then shows evidence of it in Wesley's writings. In the case of the mystery of presence, we looked first at the influence of the English Nonjurors. For the topic of remembrance, we looked at Wesley's reliance on the biblical imagery of sacrifice in the writings of Daniel Brevint. For the subject of sanctification, we examined the *Fifty Spiritual Homilies* attributed to Macarius. In each case, we followed with an examination of Wesley's writings for evidence of these influences.

This chapter follows the same method as we explore another splash of color the allegorical prism impresses upon us when holding it up to the light of Christ's presence—that of Communion as a foretaste of heaven. We will look first at a well-established historical influence on Wesley, the Moravian love feast. We will then explore how the Moravian influence finds expression in Wesleyan poetics regarding the "pledge of heaven." Then I will show how Wesley appears to have seen the communal fellowship of the love feast—experienced with sacramental overtones—as reflecting rather than replacing the power of the Eucharist. He expresses this in terms of our mutual participation in the great feast of heaven. I believe that for Wesley, the influence of the love feast found expression in eschatological language in his eucharistic hymns.

Koinonia and Agape

In the New Testament, koinonia is a scriptural concept connected to the very beginnings of our life at the table. Christianity began as a communion of the faithful who believed together and held all things in common, breaking bread in homes with glad and generous hearts. This description in Acts 2 begins with the following: "They devoted themselves to the apostle's teaching and fellowship [*koinonia* in the Greek], to the breaking of bread and the prayers."[2] Koinonia is spiritual communion, joint participation, sharing, and intimacy, an idealized state that is our deepest longing. While some interpreters of the Bible assume the agape feast described

2. Acts 2:42.

in Acts 2 was not necessarily the same as the sacrament of Holy Communion,[3] in his *Explanatory Notes*, Wesley assumes that this early Christian meal in Scripture was indeed the celebration of the sacrament. He wrote, "So their daily church communion consisted in these four particulars: 1. Hearing the word; 2. Having all things common; 3. Receiving the Lord's supper; 4. Prayer."[4]

A long history of public assemblies in Christianity has separated the sacrament in the sanctuary from the common meal in the modern-day fellowship hall. Efforts must be made to reclaim the sense of deep communion that was essential to the original, passionate practice of the church. For Wesley, the Moravian love feast did exactly that. Bowmer notes that because Wesley was steeped in Anglican tradition, practicing the Lord's Supper would have been his bounden duty. But as a result of his contact with the Moravians, he began to make it "a 'Gospel Feast' and therefore a very powerful force in the evangelical revival." In short, he claims Wesley "evangelized" the sacrament, in part because of the influence of the love feast (it was not a sacrament but nevertheless carried sacramental overtones).[5] According to Bowmer, "the Love Feast was more akin to the early Christian *agape*; food, usually biscuits, and drink, usually water, were partaken of, but there was no suggestion of consecrated elements or of a sacrificial offering." He adds, "It is possible that the enthusiasm which the Revival generated may have made the Love Feast more interesting and emotionally more satisfying than the more restrained and reverent Lord's Supper."[6] Stutzman notes that Wesley and the early Methodists held their first love feast in 1738, and this "continued to be a significant practice until the nineteenth century."[7] He quotes Wesley's journal from 1737,

---

3. Stutzman, *Recovering the Love Feast*, 31–32. He distinguishes between the tradition of the fellowship meal (koinonia) in this text and others such as 1 Cor 11 and the sacrament (anamnesis) in the Synoptic Gospels. He notes there is scholarly debate over whether these two traditions were separate or integrated in our beginnings.

4. Wesley, *Explanatory Notes*, 345.

5. Bowmer, *Sacrament*, 61.

6. Bowmer, *Sacrament*, 199.

7. Stutzman, *Recovering the Love Feast*, 158.

in which he wrote, "We joined with the Germans in one of their love-feasts. It was begun and ended with thanksgiving and prayer, and celebrated in so decent and solemn a manner as a Christian of the apostolic age would have allowed to be worthy of Christ."[8]

Of course, recovering this sense of koinonia—this communal love—is not limited to early Methodism. It finds expression in various ways throughout liturgical history. Alexander Schmemann and Paul Kachur note that "we perform, often without thinking of it, that most ancient primordial rite that from the first day of human history constituted the core of every religion; we offer a sacrifice to God."[9] For their Orthodox tradition, this offering is specifically an offering of *love*. The traditions of those who brought the bread and wine to the table in ancient liturgies evolved into the Eastern rite of the "Great Entrance," but the essence is still love.[10]

It seems clear that in early Methodist history, the love feast was a fundamental way that koinonia found ritual expression. In a separate book, Schmemann notes that "the Eucharist is the sacrament of cosmic remembrance: it is indeed a restoration of love as the very life of the world," and "the Church constitutes itself through love and on love, and in this world it is to 'witness' to Love, to re-present it, to make Love present."[11] For Wesley, the sacramental overtones of the Moravian love feast made love very present indeed. This added depth and emotional power to the celebration of Communion but did not substitute for it.

As discussed earlier, it was over the importance of regular celebration of the Eucharist that Wesley ultimately separated from the Moravians when they began to espouse a doctrine of "stillness," or quietism. This later Moravian teaching went against the grain of his Anglican heritage in its disregard for the importance of regularly partaking of the sacrament. Instead, Moravians recommended restraint from the sacrament for those who were not advanced in their spiritual journey, since it was thought that no ordinance

---

8. Stutzman, *Recovering the Love Feast*, 138.
9. Schmemann and Kachur, *Eucharist*, 101.
10. Schmemann and Kachur, *Eucharist*, 107–9.
11. Schmemann, *Life of the World*, 36.

was of any help without faith. Again, Wesley saw this teaching as an "infection" within the Moravian movement, and he and others withdrew.[12] For Wesley, the regular practice of Communion was a "very powerful instrument of religious revival,"[13] and he thought of it as "the highest form of devotion and the most comprehensive act of worship the Church could offer."[14] In short, the love-feast tradition did not substitute for the Lord's Supper, nor would Wesley allow it to contribute to the impression that the sacrament was optional. For Wesley, it enhanced the Eucharist's importance. Biographies of early Methodist preachers reveal a "reverence for the Sacrament hardly expected from such fiery evangelists."[15] Whaling argues that the Wesleyan eucharistic hymns as a whole are a "partial reaction to Moravian quietism."[16]

The Love Feast and Eschatology

It seems rather clear that the Moravian love feast had a heavy influence on Wesley's eucharistic theology. For Wesley, the experience of koinonia in community was passionately evangelistic, drawing people to a lifelong and constant hunger for the practice of the sacrament. Simply put, the early Methodists *loved* the love feast, and while at times it substituted for Communion on the frontier when clergy were not available, it enlivened rather than diminished the power of the Eucharist. As with Schmemann, for Wesley, the essence of the Eucharist is love.

How did the influence of the Moravian love feast on Wesley's theology of koinonia find expression in Wesleyan hymns? To be honest, at first glance, it is a theme that seems to be absent. It is here that I would like to make the claim that the mystery of deep communion with one another takes poetic form in the eschatological

---

12. Bowmer, *Sacrament*, 38–39.
13. Bowmer, *Sacrament*, 186.
14. Bowmer, *Sacrament*, 189.
15. Bowmer, *Sacrament*, 193.
16. Whaling, *John and Charles Wesley*, 28. For an extensive discussion of this claim, see 26–34.

Foretaste of Heaven

imagery of the hymns of the Wesley brothers ("eschatology" is, of course, related to the end-times and the final destiny of the soul and all of humanity).

Bowmer notes that the Wesleyan eucharistic hymns "do not limit heaven to the place and time assigned to it in popular thought; to Wesley heaven was timeless, present as well as future. There was much 'realized eschatology' as the early Methodists gathered round the Lord's table."[17] I tend to agree. More specifically, I see the gathering of the assembly around a meal of agape love—to once again quote the hymn from later Methodist tradition—as a "foretaste of glory divine."[18]

Bowmer shows that the section of the Wesley brothers' collection of eucharistic hymns entitled "*The SACRAMENT a Pledge of HEAVEN*" related to their "belief that the Lord's Supper is a foretaste of the heavenly banquet."[19] I suggest that Wesley's focus on eschatological imagery is quite intentional.

The first verse of the very first hymn in the third section of eucharistic hymns under the heading "*The SACRAMENT a Pledge of HEAVEN*" sings clearly of the relationship between koinonia and eschatology:

> COME let us join with one Accord
> Who share the Supper of the LORD,
> > Our LORD and Master's Praise to sing,
> Nourish'd on Earth with living Bread
> We now are at his Table fed,
> > But wait to see our Heavenly King;
> To see the great Invisible
> Without a Sacramental Veil,
> > With all his Robes of Glory on,
> In rapt'rous Joy and Love and Praise
> Him to behold with open Face,
> > High on His Everlasting Throne.[20]

---

17. Bowmer, *Sacrament*, 184.

18. Fanny Crosby, "Blessed Assurance," in The United Methodist Church, *United Methodist Hymnal*, no. 369.

19. Bowmer, *Sacrament*, 145.

20. Wesley and Wesley, *Lord's Supper*, 81.

The beginning of the last verse of this hymn continues the theme with phrases such as "Ev'n now the Marriage-Feast we share, / Ev'n now we by the Lamb are fed, / Our LORD's celestial Joy we prove, / Led by the Spirit of his love."[21] We are fed at the table in the here and now, and yet we wait with great anticipation of coming glory, all of this *led* by God's Spirit of love.

Another hymn, which is found not in the eschatological collection but in the section called "*As it is a Sign and a Means of Grace*," sings:

> Nourish us to that awful Day
> When Types and Veils shall pass away,
>   And perfect Grace in Glory end;
> Us for the Marriage-feast prepare,
> Unfurl thy Banner in the Air,
>   And bid thy Saints to Heaven ascend.[22]

We are being nourished *to* that day, and as we feast, we are *preparing* for the great marriage feast that whisks us into heaven. In the second hymn in the eschatological section, the Wesleys plainly call this a "Soul-transporting Feast" when, in remembrance, "We with thy Love are fill'd."[23] Again, in another hymn, the Wesleys ask, "Whither should our full Souls aspire / At this transporting Feast? / They never can on Earth be higher, / Or more completely blest."[24] The sacrament fills and blesses us now with the closest experience we can have of heaven on earth. The hymn continues, "To Heav'n the Mystic Banquet leads, / Let us to Heaven ascend." For the Wesleys, this feast clearly ushers us to heaven—or better yet, gives us a taste of it: "How glorious is the Life above, / Which in this Ordinance we *taste*." This same hymn continues, "The Light of Life eternal darts / Into our Souls a dazling Ray, / A Drop of Heav'n o'erflows our Hearts, / And deluges the House of Clay."[25] Not only

---

21. Wesley and Wesley, *Lord's Supper*, 82.
22. Wesley and Wesley, *Lord's Supper*, 33.
23. Wesley and Wesley, *Lord's Supper*, 82.
24. Wesley and Wesley, *Lord's Supper*, 86.
25. Wesley and Wesley, *Lord's Supper*, 87.

Foretaste of Heaven

do we "taste and see," as Ps 34:8 reminds us. For the Wesleys, we taste and are transported. We are ushered into the feast of heaven, not as an otherworldly escape from life but as a transformation of our hearts, filled by love. For Wesley, this is realized eschatology indeed. Perhaps the eschatological overtones of our koinonia for Wesley are most succinctly expressed in Hymn 108:

> For all that Joy which now we taste
>   Our happy hallow'd Souls prepare,
> O let us hold the Earnest fast,
>   This Pledge that we thy Heaven shall share,
> Shall drink it New with Thee above
> The Wine of thy Eternal Love.[26]

So, for the Wesleys, we hold the feast to taste the joy of things to come, to drink the "wine of eternal love." I propose that the koinonia experienced in the love feast, which for Wesley mirrored the essence of love in the sacrament itself, found expression in what is fundamentally eschatological language in their eucharistic hymns. Life at the table is more than confirmation of the promise of heaven; it is an experience of it in the midst of community. This is in keeping with the observations of Stevick, who saw this eschatological theme as rather unique to Wesley. He finds no real parallel in Brevint's preface, saying that the theme "is one that Wesley made his own and in which he developed several emphases." For Wesley, the table is not only a preview of things to come but a place where heaven and earth meet: "Brevint had said clearly enough that the sacrament points to 'the glory to come,' but he lacked the visual or auditory imagination to depict that glory as Wesley does."[27]

Stevick notes that for Wesley, the Eucharist makes not only the past but also the future into a present reality, holding both past and future in the "now" of faith. It is a "present act which claims the future."[28] "The sacrament is not only a pledge of heaven to come, it

---

26. Wesley and Wesley, *Lord's Supper*, 92.
27. Stevick, *Altar's Fire*, 147.
28. Stevick, *Altar's Fire*, 128–29.

Something Happens Here

brings heaven here and now." He adds, "The Supper brings heaven near, and it transports communicants to heaven itself."[29]

In Wesley's notes on the New Testament, he remarks on Jesus' words in Luke 22:16 on the last meal he would eat with them before it was fulfilled. Wesley says, "The kingdom of God did not properly commence until his resurrection. Then was fulfilled what was typified in the Passover."[30] I believe that if we were talking with Wesley today, he might add that the kingdom that commenced will one day be consummated, and the koinonia found at the table is where both the present and future kingdom meet. Stevick notes that the word "love" appears in the eucharistic hymns 120 times, and "the reality of love occupies a strategic place in the structure of the hymns, suggesting its place in Wesley's thought . . . The Lord's Supper is a place where love meets love."[31] Love is what ushers in, and what we are ushered into, at the table. As Schmemann says, "It is indeed the *preface* of the world to come, the door into the Kingdom: and this we confess and proclaim when, speaking of the Kingdom *which is to come*, we affirm that God *has already endowed us with it*. This future has been given to us in the past that it may constitute the very *present*, the life itself, now, of the Church."[32]

In my studies, I have concluded that for Wesley, the mysterious presence of Christ in the Eucharist is experienced anew *both* in connecting with the sacrifice Christ made in the past and in tasting of the promise of heavenly glory. For Wesley, the table binds the past and future together in the present-day experience of koinonia. Both themes are clearly expressed in Wesleyan hymnody. This may be one reason that in Wesley's *Explanatory Notes*, he makes no distinction between agape meals in the Scriptures and the sacrament. We saw this above regarding Acts 2, and the same is true in his notes on the Emmaus story. Next to Luke 24:35,

---

29. Stevick, *Altar's Fire*, 138.
30. Wesley, *Explanatory Notes*, 245.
31. Stevick, *Altar's Fire*, 125.
32. Schmemann, *Life of the World*, 39; italics in the original.

Foretaste of Heaven

when Christ was made known in the breaking of bread, he simply added "The Lord's Supper."[33]

The eschatological implications of the meal are extremely significant for Wesleyan Communion spirituality. Saliers, whose underlying conviction is that worship is an eschatological art, applies his presupposition to the table in particular. In discussing the tension between the experience of human life and the self-giving love of God, he says, "Indeed, we find this juxtaposition at the very heart of the holy meal: blessing and thanking God for bread and wine, which contain the hurt and suffering of the world condensed into one human life: 'my body given for you, my blood shed for you.'"[34] Time is, in a way, condensed at the table in the experience of koinonia itself. He adds, "Thus a permanent tension is created, not simply between the 'already' and the 'not yet' of the Kingdom in some large sense, but in the actualities of the concrete, specific assembly of Christians about the word and the table . . . Communion is a foretaste of glory divine."[35]

Beatrice Bruteau elaborates on the eschatological nature of the holy meal, suggesting that Jesus introduces a "new paradigm for humanity" in the sacrament of Holy Communion. This leads to an evolved "communion consciousness" that redefines persons as "transcendent, outpouring energy that indwells in all other persons, so that the energy-exchange unites the many into one and forms a new being."[36] Wesley would be in harmony with her neo-feminist perspective. Our life at the table ushers in the kingdom of God, experienced in the love found in Bruteau's "communion consciousness," in which "we will discover that we can freely and consciously 'indwell' every other person and that every other person 'indwells' us."[37] The table is, for Wesley, a way of experienc-

---

33. Wesley, *Explanatory Notes*, 255.
34. Saliers, *Worship as Theology*, 25.
35. Saliers, *Worship as Theology*, 60.
36. Bruteau, *Grand Option*, 50.
37. Bruteau, *Grand Option*, 55.

ing the "pledge of heaven" in the present reality of human life and love.[38] This is the intersection of koinonia and eschatology.

Perhaps one Wesleyan hymn summarizes this the best, noting that the oneness of the "undivided bread" that we truly are not only ties us together in Christ's love but will do so ever more closely in heaven:

> How happy are thy Servants, LORD,
>   Who thus remember Thee!
> What Tongue can tell our sweet Accord,
>   Our perfect Harmony!
>
> Who thy Mysterious Supper share,
>   Here at thy Table fed,
> Many, and yet but One we are,
>   One undivided Bread.
>
> One with the Living Bread Divine
>   Which now by Faith we eat,
> Our Hearts, and Minds, and Spirits join,
>   And all in JESUS meet.
>
> So dear the Tie where Souls agree
>   In JESU'S Dying Love;
> Then only can it closer be
>   When all are join'd above.[39]

So far, we have seen that in Wesleyan thought, the mystery of Christ's presence in the Communion gathering shimmers with three identifiable arrays of color, and we have explored them in turn. We first observed Wesley's view of remembrance, for he believed that Christ's sacrifice is experienced anew as we offer ourselves at the table. We then elaborated on Wesley's Eastern sense of personal sanctification, illuminated by the perspective of the Macarian *Homilies* he loved so much. Finally, we observed Wesley's unique way of seeing the mystery of being in deep communion with one another as a feast of love in light of the kingdom of God. For Wesley, the "real"

38. Wesley and Wesley, *Lord's Supper*, 81.
39. Wesley and Wesley, *Lord's Supper*, 138.

Foretaste of Heaven

presence of Christ in virtue, power, and effect brings the sacrificial gift of Christ to life, grows us personally toward being perfected in love, and shapes us into community as people of God gathered in light of a radical future. For Wesley, the presence of Christ meets us at the table and engages us. Just as the sacrifice of the past is connected with the offering of the present, the fellowship of the present is connected with the great feast of the future.

Real Community and a Radical Table

My favorite quote of Dietrich Bonhoeffer might be the one found in *Life Together* where he says, "Christian brotherhood is not an ideal we must realize; it is rather a reality created by God in Christ in which we may participate."[40] I am learning from a lifetime of church work that while we can't manufacture true community, we can begin to live into it. In fact, we must. This is the participation in the life of God that the table invites us into.

For community to be real, our focus must be on what pulls us forward and binds us together, not what we disagree on. This is hard right now. When we come to an impasse, the call of Holy Communion is to come back to the table and work it out instead of going our separate ways. When we can't imagine moving forward together, the lens of Communion gives us the opportunity to let God reenvision and refashion us. In divisive times, disagreements have led to entrenched requirements that people on the "other side" see it our way, or at least follow our rules . . . or we simply take our toys and go play somewhere else. How typical of North American culture these days, but the table compels us to be different than the world.

What does it mean to be in real community, daring to participate in this new reality Bonhoeffer speaks of? Disagreement has always been part of the story of denominations and faith movements. Yet, by the grace of God, the Spirit ushers in and messes with us, even in the midst of the mess we make of ourselves.

---

40. Bonhoeffer, *Life Together*, 30.

Something Happens Here

Rev. Dr. Martin Luther King Jr. famously said, "We shall overcome because the arc of the moral universe is long, but it bends toward justice."[41] As I have revisited the Gospels and the book of Acts in recent years, examining Jesus and the early church in their repeatedly bold actions on behalf of gentiles and Samaritans, I have come to the conclusion that the arc of Christian history is also long, but it bends toward inclusion. Yes, there are difficult practical matters to work out in this moment of impasse in the United Methodist Church. But as people of the table, we are willing to do what it takes in the messiness of what it means to be in community together. First and foremost, we must focus on following Christ. After that, we may need to decentralize decisions we can't agree on corporately and allow for contextualized ministry, trusting in the workings of the Holy Spirit. It seems to me this is the only way forward for the United Methodist Church, unless the definition of being God's church is that we must be like-minded thinkers and like-minded actors. As I have said before, how conspicuous that the culture wars that threaten to splinter us apart are over matters that are not even mentioned in the Gospels or the ancient creeds.

The United Methodist Church and our predecessors have made it through divisive issues such as slavery, voting rights, temperance, civil rights, and ordaining women. It is the most evenly widespread denomination in the United States, so there will always be cultural issues to sort through. But this is a moment where we must decide whether to stay at the table and work it out or not, and to me, that's the very definition of church.

John Wesley said, in his sermon "Catholic Spirit," "Though we cannot think alike, may we not love alike? May we not be of one heart, though we are not of one opinion? Without all doubt, we may."[42] He also said, in his sermon "On Schism," that "it is evil in itself. To separate from a body of living Christians with whom we were before united is a grievous breach of the law of love," and hence it "is only when our love grows cold that we can consider separation." He continues, "The pretenses for separation may be

---

41. Washington, *Testament of Hope*, 277.
42. Outler and Heitzenrater, *John Wesley's Sermons*, 301.

innumerable, but want of love is always the real cause; otherwise, they would still hold the unity of the Spirit in the bond of peace."[43]

The table is a radical table, because it brings us back to what connects us, which is not agreement or like-minded thinking but community and *love-minded* thinking. We are bound by our belief, yes, but I'm reminded that in early English, the word "belief" was pronounced "by life." How we love those we don't agree with is the very definition of Christian fellowship.

There's a reason the meal in Jesus' life and ministry was a bold political statement, a matter of God's redefinition of who's in and who's out. The second-biggest criticism Jesus got, besides the claim that he is the Son of God, is that he ate with "sinners." For Jesus, mealtime was a daring declaration. It still is.

Inclusiveness is much more than everybody in the room being "allowed" at the table. Inclusivity is not ultimately about the present situation at all; it's about the kingdom of God ushering in. We gather in the present moment, in light of the future and not in the shadows of the past. Being in community is not about you and me but about the feast of heaven we participate in. The parable of the great feast makes it crystal clear that God is radically inclusive.

I realize there are difficult things to work out regarding rites of marriage and ordination, and this is not easy work. But sadly, it appears that what the world sees in the institution right now is not spiritual discernment but intolerance. Segments of the church on both the far right and the far left may come across to the world as Pharisees, straining gnats and swallowing camels.[44] There are some that argue that Wesley, in this very same sermon "On Schism," ultimately recognized that there are times when we cannot be blamed for separating, if "we could not continue without sin."[45] This is, of course, true, and it is hard to refute the example Wesley found in the Protestant Reformation. Some United Methodists are offended by those that protest as a way of working against the rules in the *United Methodist Book of Discipline*, and others are offended by

---

43. Wesley, *Sermons*, 285.
44. Matt 23:24.
45. Wesley, *Sermons*, 287.

those who work hard to tighten those rules. I truly believe all these are faithful Christians trying to live as a covenant community as best they can. However, I wonder if those who have become intent on leaving the main body are as concerned about their own sin as their perception of the sin in others. It appears we are finding difficulty trusting followers of Christ to rigorously work out their ethics in light of Scripture, tradition, reason, and experience. When the effort becomes about instituting this theological task for everyone else, we will only find that ultimately, we can not. Wesley continued, in his sermon "On Schism": "As such a separation is evil in itself, being a breach of brotherly love, so it brings forth evil fruit; it is naturally productive of the most mischievous consequences. It opens a door to all unkind tempers, both in ourselves and others."[46] I'm afraid it has.

True community is messy. If I must make a choice, I choose to be part of the chaos of community rather than not be in communion at all. If we let culture war issues drive a wedge between us, what will the next one be? Should we not choose love even when it's hard to love? Fortunately, Jesus never said that we had to agree on everything. What he did say was this: "By this everyone will know that you are my disciples, if you have love for one another."[47]

---

46. Wesley, *Sermons*, 286.
47. John 13:35.

6

Grand Channel of Grace

I GREW UP IN a pastor's family, and when I was ten years old, my father led a youth retreat for our local church. It was held at a beautiful place called Camp Lee in Anniston, Alabama. Since Dad was the pastor, I got to go, even though I was not old enough for youth group. I remember sitting in the laps of some of the teenage girls. That made quite an impression on me! But more than that, I remember the kids in the youth group talking about their relationship with God in their own language, and it connected with me in ways my Sunday school teachers didn't. It did more than impress me . . . it touched me.

I asked my dad toward the end of the retreat if I could say something at the closing service. Without even asking what it was, he called on me at the close of vespers the next day in the beautiful outdoor prayer chapel on Camp Lee's property. I remember it like it was yesterday. I said, "I've grown up in a good family. All my life, I've been going to Sunday school and Vacation Bible School, and I've learned the stories of Jesus. But this weekend, I have realized that Jesus is more than just a storybook character. He's real. And I want everybody to know that I am going to serve him with my whole life."

Something Happens Here

I had no idea at the time that I would become a preacher. I'm glad God didn't reveal that to me yet ... I might have run the other way! My life has certainly not been a perfect adventure. But I have held that moment in my sacred memory. What I did not realize for many years was that in my own ten-year-old way, I was articulating John Wesley's teachings on grace.

As I mentioned in an earlier chapter, Wesley had a very special way of talking about grace, the free gift of love God has for us, both unearned and undeserved. He called the pervasive effect of God's grace on us the "way of salvation" and describes it as prevenient, justifying, and sanctifying grace. Prevenient grace is that gracious initiative that moves before our human efforts, works even when we can't see it, and woos us into relationship with God; prevenient grace is what I was describing when I said, "I've grown up in a good family. All my life, I've been going to Sunday school and Vacation Bible School, and I've learned the stories of Jesus." Justifying grace is the grace of God that is experienced when our relationship with God is restored, we are realigned with God's gracious gift of new life, and we have assurance of forgiveness. This is what I was getting at when I said, "But this weekend, I have realized that Jesus is more than just a storybook character. He's real." Sanctifying grace is that freely given gift of God that continually restores us into the fullness of Christ's image, as Paul spoke of when he said, "And all of us, with unveiled faces, seeing the glory of the Lord as though reflected in a mirror, are being transformed into the same image from one degree of glory to another; for this comes from the Lord, the Spirit."[1] That's what I was articulating when I said, "And I want everybody to know that I am going to serve him with my whole life." I had no idea at the time that I was so thoroughly Wesleyan, for he saw this as our "way of salvation." For Wesley, we experience the way of salvation and the pervasive nature of grace through the "means of grace," gifts God has given us for grace to be poured into our lives.

---

1. 2 Cor 3:18.

Grand Channel of Grace

The Means of Grace and the "Grand Channel"

Our method of exploration so far has been visualized by the idea of holding up Communion like a prism to the light of Wesley's view of the mystery of Christ's presence in Communion, and then observing the array of colors in Wesley's eucharistic thought that emerge—the remembrance of Christ's sacrifice in our offering of ourselves, the sanctification of the soul through Christian perfection, and the experience of community that ushers in the feast of heaven. I would like to turn us to the Wesleyan fusion of these ideas that is uniquely expressed in his assertion that Communion is a "means of grace." For Wesley, this is the defining mystery of the sacrament.

While the phrase "means of grace" certainly does not originate with Wesley, it clearly capsulates his Communion theology. Wesley's most explicit introduction to this idea is found in his sermon with that very title: "The Means of Grace." In discussing 1 Cor 11, he says:

> And that this is also an ordinary stated means of receiving the grace of God is evident from those words of the Apostle which occur in the preceding chapter: "The cup of blessing which we bless, is it not the communion (or communication) of the blood of Christ? The bread which we break, is it not the communion of the body of Christ?" (1 Cor. 10:16). Is not the eating of the bread and the drinking of that cup, the outward and visible means whereby God conveys to our souls all that spiritual grace, that righteousness, and peace, and joy in the Holy Ghost which were purchased by the body of Christ once broken, and the blood of Christ once shed for us? Let all, therefore, who truly desire the grace of God, eat of that bread and drink of that cup.[2]

In this sermon, the definition of a means of grace is a "channel through which the grace of God is conveyed,"[3] and the term applies to activities such as the spiritual disciplines in such a way that de-emphasizes human action and places focus on the initiative of God.

2. Outler and Heitzenrater, *John Wesley's Sermons*, 165.
3. Outler and Heitzenrater, *John Wesley's Sermons*, 167.

Something Happens Here

But Communion is not merely *one* of the channels for Wesley; it is the "grand channel."[4] In "Upon our Lord's Sermon On the Mount, IV," he preaches on the phrase "Give us this day our daily bread," saying that "it was the judgment of many of the ancient Fathers that we are here to *understand* the sacramental bread also; daily received in the beginning by the whole church of Christ, and highly esteemed till the love of many waxed cold, as the grand channel whereby the grace of the Spirit was conveyed to all the souls of the children of God."[5] This idea of Holy Communion as the "grand channel" finds its way into Wesleyan hymnody, where "In all the Channels of thy Grace, / I still have Fellowship with Thee, / But chiefly here my Soul is fed / With Fullness of Immortal Bread."[6]

There is some debate over Wesley's view of the role of human response to this grace. In the sermon "The Duty of Constant Communion," he says, "He has given us certain means of obtaining his help. One of these is the Lord's Supper, which of his infinite mercy he hath given for this very end: that through this means we may be assisted to attain those blessings which he hath prepared for us; that we may obtain holiness on earth and everlasting glory in heaven."[7] For Gregory Neal, Wesley's language leads to the conclusion that there is a distinction between the Eucharist and other means of grace in that human response is fundamental to completing the work of Communion. Recognizing that "it must first be noted that the principal actor in *every* means of grace is God," he finds that "the sacraments differ from the other means of grace, however, when it comes to our response in faith."[8] Neal argues that for the means of grace to be completed within the sacrament, a response of faith must be forthcoming: "The sacraments not only communicate to us effectively God's grace, but when we partake of them by faith they complete a work of God's sanctification within us. Our response of faith is required for the grace to 'move us on toward perfection.'

---

4. Whaling, *John and Charles Wesley*, 116.
5. Outler and Heitzenrater, *John Wesley's Sermons*, 232.
6. Wesley and Wesley, *Lord's Supper*, 39.
7. Outler and Heitzenrater, *John Wesley's Sermons*, 505.
8. Neal, *Grace upon Grace*, 52–53.

Without our *response*, the sacraments are still a means of grace, but they are not *completed*—they are not actualized."[9]

I find Neal's concept of a "completed" sacrament as an additive to Wesley; it would seem that if this were the teaching of Wesley, then Wesley would have said it himself. His language of "attaining" and "obtaining" grace is best interpreted to mean the act of *receiving* the gift of grace, not completing the work of it.

In any case, for Wesley, the Eucharist is the "grand channel" of grace indeed. The Articles of Religion, adopted from the Church of England and edited for Methodism by Wesley himself, read, "Sacraments ordained of Christ are not only badges or tokens of Christian men's profession, but rather they are certain signs of grace, and God's good will toward us, by which he doth work invisibly in us, and doth not only quicken, but also strengthen and confirm, our faith in him."[10] This assertion that even our faith response is the invisible work of grace offers a corrective to Neal's interpretation.

The "Grand Channel" in the Hymns

Such careful discernment regarding Wesley's theology of Communion as the "grand channel," or the greatest of the means of grace, leads us back to survey additional eucharistic hymns. In the second section of the collection under the heading *"As it is a Sign and a Means of Grace"* is one of his more well-known Communion hymns:

> O Thou who this Mysterious Bread
>   Didst in *Emmaus* break,
> Return, herewith our Souls to feed,
>   And to thy Followers speak.
>
> Unseal the Volume of thy Grace,
>   Apply the Gospel-word,
> Open our Eyes to see thy Face,
>   Our Hearts to know the LORD.

---

9. Neal, *Grace upon Grace*, 54.
10. *United Methodist Book*, 69 (Articles of Religion, Article XVI).

Something Happens Here

> Of Thee we commune still, and mourn
>   Till Thou the Veil remove;
> Talk with us, and our Hearts shall burn
>   With Flames of fervent Love.
>
> Inkindle now the heavenly Zeal,
>   And make thy Mercy known,
> And give our Pardon'd Souls to feel
>   That GOD and Love are One.[11]

Here we clearly see the vivid colors, discussed in previous chapters, displayed in his theology of Communion as a means of grace. Encountering, in effect, the presence of Christ in the sacrament by personally entering into the Emmaus narrative, the Wesleys ask the one who broke the "mysterious bread" to feed our souls and speak truth to our hearts, unsealing the "volume" of God's grace. The singer prays that God open our eyes and hearts and that our hearts then burn with flames of love. For Wesley, this meal is a means of grace indeed when Christ shows up and reveals his presence. It is a meal where he sanctifies our souls with an encounter with the Word, as he did on the road to Emmaus. It is a meal that leads the heart to a love that enkindles "heavenly zeal" with an eye on the great feast. In short, this one hymn draws together the colors discussed in this book in its vivid imagery, with only Wesley's unique use of sacrificial and offering imagery lacking.

You might have noticed that there is no reference in this hymn to the effects of human effort aside from the one reference to communing itself, and even here, the act of receiving is done in mourning until the "veil" is removed. This reflects very careful attention on the part of the Wesleys and reflects the influence of the Eastern view of the mingling of grace and free will. Ours is to be attentive to the painter, to be still and receive. In short, Communion is not an ordinance for Wesley—something we do as an act of obedience, or as a contribution to our salvation, or even as some sort of "completion" of love being made perfect in us. It is

---

11. Wesley and Wesley, *Lord's Supper*, 22–23.

purely a means of grace. The first eucharistic hymn in this section calls it "the glorious Instrument Divine."[12]

Another eucharistic hymn in this section is worthy of great attention because it makes reference to one of the Nonjuror usages, the mixture of wine and water. The hymn interprets this mingling as a sign of both atonement and sanctification. The imagery specifies how, for Wesley, Communion serves as a means of grace to both redeem and to make holy. A portion sings:

> By Water and by Blood redeem,
> And wash us in the mingled Stream.
>
> The Sin-atoning Blood apply,
> And let the Water sanctify,
> Pardon and Holiness impart,
> Sprinkle and purify our Heart,
> Wash out the last Remains of Sin,
> And make our inmost Nature clean.
>
> The double Stream in Pardon rolls,
> And brings thy Love into our Souls . . .[13]

This "double stream" of wine and water mingled together is a means of grace indeed, bringing both pardon and sanctification. The imagery in the hymn reflects a synthesis of several of the themes considered above. It brings the sacrifice of Christ to life in the present ("Sin-atoning Blood"), it grants sanctifying grace through our struggles ("Holiness impart, / Sprinkle and purify our Heart"), and it pours the love of God into our souls.

Another hymn sings of the sanctification that comes by God's gracious initiative, feeding and training us for heaven with "fresh supplies of love" until we behold the mystery of God one day:

> AUTHOR of Life Divine,
>   Who hast a Table spread,
> Furnish'd with Mystick Wine
> And everlasting Bread,

12. Wesley and Wesley, *Lord's Supper*, 22.
13. Wesley and Wesley, *Lord's Supper*, 24.

> Preserve the Life Thyself hast given,
> And feed, and train us up for Heaven.
>
> Our needy Souls sustain
>   With fresh Supplies of Love,
> Till all thy Life we gain,
>   And all thy Fulness prove,
> And, strength'ned by thy perfect Grace,
> Behold without a Veil thy Face.[14]

There is a sense here that we are being nourished toward heaven and strengthened only by grace toward perfection in love when we behold the face of God—a theme that resonates with Macarian thought. This veil imagery is picked up in a hymn with eschatological overtones discussed earlier:

> Nourish us to that awful Day
> When Types and Veils shall pass away,
>   And perfect Grace in Glory end;
> Us for the Marriage-feast prepare,
> Unfurl thy Banner in the Air,
>   And bid thy Saints to Heaven ascend.[15]

Here, the image of the Lord's Supper as the great wedding feast we are drawn into is quite prominent, though this hymn's inclusion in the section on the "means of grace" magnifies its emphasis on the grace of God removing the veil and perfecting us. Another hymn sings, "Bless with the Blessings of thy Throne, / and perfect all our Souls in One."[16] Yet another sings:

> Then, then let us see
> Thy Glory, and be
> Caught up in the Air
> This Heavenly Supper in Heaven to share.[17]

---

14. Wesley and Wesley, *Lord's Supper*, 30.
15. Wesley and Wesley, *Lord's Supper*, 33.
16. Wesley and Wesley, *Lord's Supper*, 37.
17. Wesley and Wesley, *Lord's Supper*, 80.

Grand Channel of Grace

Again, there is an eschatological motif that comes with our longing for Christian perfection as a response (and no more than a response) to sanctifying grace. We do not achieve perfection . . . there is no "spiritual ladder" here. At best, we are "caught up in the air" and ushered into the great feast. As Saliers says, the deepest mystery of all is that "worship is participation in God's very life."[18]

We have discussed the theology Wesley articulated on Communion as a "means of grace." We have highlighted various themes from our study that appear to be painted into the hymns of the specific section of the Wesleyan eucharistic hymn collection entitled "*As it is a Sign and a Means of Grace.*" There seems to be evidence that this doctrine synthesizes the beautiful colors of Wesley's distinctive thoughts on the Eucharist. There are references in the hymns to Wesley's belief in encountering the presence of the risen Christ, in remembrance that brings sacrificial imagery to life in the present, in the sanctification of the soul that purifies our love, and in the mingling of grace and free will in our journey toward Christian perfection. There are also references to the eschatological theme of being drawn into the great feast. These are the various ways Wesley sees Communion as "unsealing the volume" of grace.

There is one additional observation I'd like to make. In seeing Communion as a "means of grace," Wesley is careful to give attention to both personal sanctification and corporate edification. This reflects both the influence of the Eastern tradition on his sense of theosis and the influence of the Moravian love feast, but the distinction is noticeably intentional. One hymn sings of a very personal, emotive experience:

> How He did these Creatures raise,
>   And make this Bread and Wine
> Organs to convey his Grace
>   To this poor Soul of mine,
> I cannot the Way descry,
>   Need not know the Mystery;
> Only this I know that I
>   Was blind, but now I see.[19]

18. Saliers, *Worship as Theology*, 48.
19. Wesley and Wesley, *Lord's Supper*, 43.

Another, on the other hand, sings of nourishment that strengthens the entire community:

> Thy Flesh for our Support is given,
> Thou art the Bread sent down from Heaven,
> > That all Mankind by Thee might live;
> O that we evermore may prove
> The Manna of thy quick'ning Love,
> > And all thy Life of Grace receive![20]

So, for Wesley, life at the table is a "means of grace" that sanctifies and edifies, that pours love into the hearts of God's people and shapes the community in grace. Yet perhaps the best concluding summary of his theology regarding the Eucharist as a "means of grace" is found in Hymn 66, which draws us back to our starting place with Wesley's Nonjuror influence:

> JESU, my LORD and GOD bestow
> All which thy Sacrament doth show,
> > And make real the Sign
> A sure effectual Means of Grace,
> > Then sanctify my Heart and bless,
> And make it all like thine.
>
> Great is thy Faithfulness and Love,
> Thine Ordinance can never prove
> > Of none Effect and vain,
> Only do Thou my Heart prepare,
> To find thy Real Presence there,
> > And all thy Fullness gain.[21]

For Neal, the Methodist approach to the Communion table follows Wesley in affirming "that the presence of Jesus Christ is *real* but refuses to adopt any particular way, mechanism, or theory as to how his presence is real—it simply *is*."[22] This real presence is the *source* of grace in the sacrament, and sharing the meal is the *means* of grace in the sacrament. Echoing Brevint's words in the

---

20. Wesley and Wesley, *Lord's Supper*, 33.
21. Wesley and Wesley, *Lord's Supper*, 48.
22. Neal, *Grace upon Grace*, 107.

preface to the eucharistic hymn collection,[23] Wesley calls it the "effectual means" of grace. As we have seen, for Wesley, the presence of Christ as we gather for the meal brings to present experience the sacrificial love of Jesus. It nourishes, purifies, and sanctifies the soul in its journey of "moving on to perfection" in love, and it edifies the church in light of the great feast of God's kingdom. Stevick adds, "Wesley and his tradition held that the Sacrament of the Table is both a witness to grace once given and also a present enactment of grace."[24] This is Wesley's theology of the "means of grace" in a nutshell. As Brevint, after a vivid discussion of bread being beaten by hand as a way of reexperiencing the bruising of Christ, put it: "Thus this Sacrament alone represents at once, both what our LORD suffer'd, and what he still doth for us."[25] As I have said, something happens here. It happens both in the personal experience of the communicant and in the corporate experience of the faith community. Communion is the "grand channel" by which this grace effects and changes us.

It's Not Something You "Do"

We live in a world of doing, performing, functioning, and succeeding. At least in North American culture, productivity is what we most admire. We set our athletes and performers on such high pedestals that they sometimes fall. Even in the church, we tend to affirm others for how busy they are rather than looking for what Paul called the "fruit of the Spirit" (Gal 5:22). We exalt our flagship churches for the large buildings and the big crowds they accomplish, and yet not all of them take what I call the "theological plunge."

Communion is the "grand channel" for experiencing life in a different way. In part, this is because of one of the things I have often said—worship is not something you *do*. It's something you *join*. We join in the songs of all creation and the praises of the

---

23. Introduction in Wesley and Wesley, *Lord's Supper*, 16.
24. Stevick, *Altar's Fire*, 164.
25. Daniel Brevint, preface to Wesley and Wesley, *Lord's Supper*, 11.

communion of saints across space and time, and Communion is the most vivid act of worship that draws us into something bigger than we are. In addition, this is because Communion is an invitation into the very life of God.

I have heard a few pastors say, "Religion is about what we *do*. Christianity is about what Christ has *done*." That is both simply and beautifully put. When we "do" church and we become so very hyper-focused (in these times of great discord) on how everybody else can or can't "do" church, we can so easily become the very Pharisees Jesus stood up to. Thankfully, Communion is not something we do but something we are invited to—or better yet, invited *into*. As a sacrament, it is an outward and visible sign of an inward and spiritual grace. Other traditions think of it fundamentally as an ordinance, a matter of obedience. But not United Methodists.

One of my favorite passages of Scripture is the call of the first disciples according to the book of John. I'm intrigued at how the phrase "Come and see" appears twice. First, it is what Jesus says to his brand-new disciples when John the Baptist sends some of his own to follow Jesus. Jesus asks the probing question "What are you looking for?" As if to skirt the issue, they answer with their own question: "Where are you staying?" Jesus answers, "Come and see."[26]

Part of what I love about this passage is that the words of Jesus are spiritually formative. Later in the chapter, when Philip is inviting Nathaniel to follow Jesus and Nathaniel is skeptical about anything good coming from Nazareth, Philip, already following in the way of Jesus, answers in the same way: "Come and see."[27]

That's the essence of discipleship. It's not about being obedient to behavioral standards but about following the one who will show us the way as we go. Again, it's not about rules but about *relationship*. Communion is the "grand channel" of grace, as Wesley put it, because it is the central way Christ continues to invite us to "come and see." To summarize this book so far, Communion invites us into the presence of the living Christ, a fresh experience

---

26. John 1:38–39.
27. John 1:46.

Grand Channel of Grace

of his sacrificial love, a journey into the depths of the heart, and life in the kingdom of God. That's how grace works.

Since following Jesus is always changing us and shaping us, we should notice how entrenched we can so easily become in our times of division. If indeed it's the "grand channel," we must trust in the work of God at the table. There must be less focus on our institutional brokenness, which leads us to analyze and criticize what everyone else is doing, and more focus on what Christ has done and is doing among us. Let's keep going back to the table. Going back to it together, we begin to see.

I have a pastor friend who told the people of his new-member class, "The only thing we don't tolerate here is intolerance." That sounds a lot like Jesus, who conspicuously only condemned one type of person . . . the Pharisee. It was not the ones they called "sinners" whom Jesus went toe to toe with but the very ones who had a propensity to decide which type of sinner was too unclean to come to the table and what they must do to measure up first.

7

Becoming the Body

FOR FOUR YEARS, I spent three weeks of summer intensives at the beautiful campus of Sewanee: The University of the South in Tennessee, which I affectionately call "Hogwarts on the mountain." By the third year, I was close to completing the twenty-mile Perimeter Trail around the crest of the mountain. The language of finding a "way forward" had become common in Methodist leadership circles, since we were approaching a called General Conference that was supposed to find some level of resolve over the deepening divide regarding matters of human sexuality. This annual trek was becoming a prayer walk, as I became intentional to pray about the "way forward" as I walked this path. One afternoon after class, I found myself taking a break from my routine hike to check out a natural bridge I had heard about on another part of the campus.

As I walked down the hill to look over this bridge that had developed purely out of divine initiative, I was whisked away into a mystical experience. I climbed to the top of the bridge and crossed over, pondering the concept of finding a "way forward." Jesus called himself the "way." He did not say he would show us the way, or tell us about the path, or send us on our journey, but that he *is* the way. I don't believe he said this to be exclusive, as it is often interpreted. I believe he said this to remind us that following him is a journey, and the wisdom of God is a path that will take us to new places and new spaces. Christianity is not a list of rules to follow or a set of doctrines to swallow but a relationship with the divine one who is fully embodied in the person of Christ Jesus. We did not need to build a bridge to provide a way forward. It is a gift given to us in Christ. After all, before Christians were called Christians, the movement was simply called "the Way."[1]

Just as he began his disciples' journey with the call to "follow *me*" (Matt 4:19, italics added), he intentionally prepared them for the completion of his earthly life with a meal invitation to "do this in remembrance of *me*" (Luke 22:19, italics added). As I have said, it is not a call to simply remember a meal, a liturgy, or a lesson on the meaning of the cross but to reexperience *me* . . . *all* of me. The invitation at the table completes what could be seen as a two-part calling of the disciples. Life at the table takes us much deeper into the heart of what it means to truly follow. On that natural bridge, I determined that no matter what, wherever this path took me, I would choose the way of Christ. How Christ behaved toward others is the best lens through which we interpret Scripture, even his own words. Christian spirituality is embodied spirituality, and in Christ, the "fullness of deity dwells bodily."[2] Jesus offered the invitation at the table when he knew the time was coming soon when he was no longer going to walk on earth. We were to become the hands and feet of Christ.

We Are What We Eat

I grew up in the 1970s and 1980s and can vividly remember the animated advertisements on public broadcasting television repeating the phrase "You are what you eat." I suppose I am a product of the times I grew up in, because the phrase often comes to my mind

---

1. See Acts 9:2, 11:26.
2. Col 2:9.

when sharing the Great Thanksgiving liturgy in *The United Methodist Hymnal* and *United Methodist Book of Worship*. My favorite part of the liturgy is the prayer over the bread and cup to "make them be for us the body and blood of Christ, that we might be for the world the body of Christ, redeemed by his blood."[3] We pray that we are what we eat. We pray that we become the hands and feet of Christ and walk in his "way."

We have already explored several themes that are most distinctive about Wesleyan Communion theology. Our journey began with the sense of the real presence of Christ in the gathered assembly around the table. We observed how the power of Christ's presence is, for Wesley, what invites us to experience anew the sacrifice of Christ in the offering of ourselves. We discerned how this sense of divine presence shapes our lifelong adventure of being made Christ-like through divine indwelling, being refined through our struggles, and being moved toward perfection in love, even as we encounter Christ at the table. We discussed how Christ's presence draws us to heaven and ushers in the kingdom, as our community provides a foretaste of the great feast of the family of God. Finally, I proposed that evidence of these vivid colors may be illuminated in Wesley's teaching on the Eucharist as a means of grace. In each case, I have identified historical sources of these distinctive colors and find clear evidence of them in the sung poetry, sermons, and writings of the Wesleys. Now let us turn to how this distinctiveness is vividly expressed in the Great Thanksgiving we use today.

I would like to suggest that the epiclesis, or prayer for the work of the Holy Spirit, presently recited in the United Methodist liturgy is a concise yet full expression of all these distinctive teachings of Wesleyan Communion spirituality. You may remember that the epiclesis was one of the four Nonjuror usages adopted by Wesley and discussed in a previous chapter. The word "epiclesis" comes from the Greek for "invocation," or "calling down."[4] In Communion liturgy, it is the prayer calling down the blessing of

---

3. The United Methodist Church, *Book of Worship*, 38.
4. Bradshaw and Johnson, *Eucharistic Liturgies*, 47, 121–23.

Becoming the Body

God on the assembly. The Spirit is sought "so that the gifts and/or the people may be sanctified, blessed, and made holy."[5]

The epiclesis is a complex idea in Christian history. In Roman Catholic tradition, reciting the words of institution uttered by Jesus Christ ("This is my body" and "This is my blood") was thought to be the moment when eucharistic elements change in substance and become the body and blood of Christ (a teaching called "transubstantiation"). In Eastern Orthodox tradition, the epiclesis completes the transformation of the elements into the real presence of Christ, though it is not considered a "moment" but a conclusion of a process. Lutherans teach the doctrine of consubstantiation, in which the bread and cup, rather than experiencing a change in the substance of the elements, remain as they were but are joined by an additional spiritual presence. In other Protestant traditions, the presence of Christ is seen in different ways, if there is considered to be a presence at all.[6]

For Wesley and the Methodist tradition, as we have already seen, this mysterious presence is considered "real" in that it is experienced in quality, power, and effect in the assembly of the faithful. The meal becomes, then, a means of God's grace. The key ingredient acknowledging this in the Great Thanksgiving is the epiclesis in the United Methodist liturgy, which is prayed in this way:

The pastor may hold hands, palms down, over the bread and cup.

> Pour out your Holy Spirit on us gathered here,
>   and on these gifts of bread and wine.
> Make them be for us the body and blood of Christ,
>   that we might be for the world the body of Christ,
>   redeemed by his blood.

The pastor may raise hands.

---

5. Eslinger, *Holy Mystery*, 168.

6. This is discussed at length in Bradshaw and Johnson, *Eucharistic Liturgies*, esp. 225–29, 240–49, 257–60, 265–70.

Something Happens Here

> By your Spirit, make us one with Christ,
> > one with each other,
> > > and one in ministry to all the world,
> > until Christ comes in final victory
> > > and we feast at his heavenly banquet.
>
> Through your Son Jesus Christ,
> > with the Holy Spirit in your holy Church,
> > all honor and glory is yours, almighty Father,
> > now and for ever. **Amen.**[7]

Dick Eslinger writes of his involvement in composing the actual phrasing, with an eye on the liturgies of the early church and a "primitive" (Wesley's word for "original") sense of how the presence of Christ becomes real. Yes, the language comes from both the Anglican tradition and the ecumentical Liturgical Movement of the twentieth century, which focused on the liturgies of the ancient church, especially leaning on Hippolytus from the third century.[8] Morrill reminds us, when reflecting on this ecumenical renewal, that the "real purpose [of the Eucharist] is the transformation of the participants as members of the body of Christ."[9] This transformation, experienced in what Wesley called the "grand channel" of all the means of grace, is made explicit in the liturgy.

There are five key phrases in the United Methodist prayer for the work of the Spirit that I would like to bring to light. It should not surprise us that the liturgical flow of the epiclesis itself fits neatly into the outline of this book. First, consider the opening phrase: "Pour out your Holy Spirit on us gathered here, / and on these gifts of bread and wine."[10] This prayer calling for the Spirit is, of course, what sets apart the epiclesis in the Great Thanksgiving. However, the flow of the next phrases is revealing. The emphasis is on the movement of the Spirit "on us gathered here," the divine assembly, followed by the recognition that the Spirit falls

---

7. The United Methodist Church, *Book of Worship*, 38; boldface in the original.
8. Eslinger, *Holy Mystery*, 167–74.
9. Morrill, *Encountering Christ*, 94.
10. The United Methodist Church, *Book of Worship*, 38.

Becoming the Body

on the bread and cup as well. The presence of Christ, which comes through the Holy Spirit, is most "real" when it falls on the people of God. As Saliers states, "No praying ever guarantees the presence of God, but when authentic praise and thanksgiving are offered in response to the divine initiative, the conditions for receiving the divine self-communication are made alive."[11] We are, as Lathrop reminded us in a previous chapter, the "fundamental symbol" of the presence of Christ.[12] Christ becomes present through the work of the Holy Spirit in a way that flows first and foremost into the gathering itself.

Second, let us consider the phrasing "Make them be for us the body and blood of Christ, / that we might be for the world the body of Christ, / redeemed by his blood."[13] Notice the verbs, moving from "Make them *be*" to "that we might *be*." The flow is quite revealing. As we have said, it specifies that the location of "real" presence is not only in the elements but, more importantly, in the assembly of the people. This is right in line with Wesley's understanding of remembrance, for our offering of ourselves enlivens and brings to present experience the sacrifice of Christ, made once for all time. As Brevint put it in Wesley's preface to his Communion hymns, "This Sacrifice, which by a *real* Oblation was not to be offered more than once, is by a Devout and Thankful Commemoration, to be offered up every Day," and "This Sacrament, by our Remembrance, becomes a kind of Sacrifice, whereby we present before God the Father, that precious Oblation of his Son once offered."[14] The United Methodist liturgy is also consistent with Wesley's priorities, for their hymn texts are careful not to see the Eucharist as a repetition of the sacrifice Christ made. In offering ourselves, the sacrifice is made alive, and we become the body of Christ, redeemed by his blood. This is reflected earlier in the Great Thanksgiving, after the words of institution but prior to the epiclesis, where we find these words of oblation, or offering:

11. Saliers, *Worship as Theology*, 86.
12. Lathrop, *Holy People*, 21.
13. The United Methodist Church, *Book of Worship*, 38.
14. Daniel Brevint, preface to Wesley and Wesley, *Lord's Supper*, 21.

And so,
in remembrance of these your mighty acts in Jesus Christ,
we offer ourselves in praise and thanksgiving
    as a holy and living sacrifice,
    in union with Christ's offering for us,
as we proclaim the mystery of faith.
Christ has died; Christ is risen; Christ will come again.[15]

Eslinger notes that the words above describe a representation, not a repetition, of the sacrifice of Christ.[16] As we discussed earlier, he tells an interesting story about the evolution of the phrasing of our present-day eucharistic liturgy, which, in the 1972 Service of Word and Table and other subsequent worship supplements, had the words "experience anew" for "remembrance." He remarks that these words were "so attuned to Methodist liturgical piety" and laments that they were dropped in the present 1989 *United Methodist Hymnal* and 1992 *Book of Worship*.[17] For Wesley, in remembrance, we offer *ourselves* in union with Christ's sacrifice.

Third, let us observe the words "By your Spirit, make us one with Christ."[18] This encapsulates Wesley's understanding of sanctification. Eastern spirituality is summarized in this brief prayer, for union with God in Christ is the purpose of growing in Christian perfection in the Eastern tradition that influenced Wesley so much. This union is described with more precision as divine indwelling, yes, vividly discussed in the section on the Macarian *Homilies* above. But while Macarius "understands Christianity as the renewal of the human being,"[19] for him this is not glorified self-help. It is not just becoming *like* God; it is coming into *union* with God. It is "cooperating with divine grace, in order to ascend the inner Sinai and arrive

---

15. The United Methodist Church, *Book of Worship*, 38; boldface in the original.

16. Eslinger, *Holy Mystery*, 165.

17. Eslinger, *Holy Mystery*, 154.

18. The United Methodist Church, *Book of Worship*, 38.

19. Heiromonk Alexander Golitzin, "A Testimony to Christianity as Transfiguration: The Macarian Homilies and Orthodox Spirituality," in Kimbrough, *Orthodox and Wesleyan Spirituality*, 129.

Becoming the Body

at the conscious perception, and even the vision, of the Presence."[20] I would say that it is an incomplete summary of the Eastern spirituality of *theosis* to reduce it to the concept of becoming more "Christ-like." Our prayer "Make us one with Christ"[21] sums up this longing much better. We become one with Christ as we are continually drawn into his life and refined in his love. Communion is the grand channel of grace that nourishes us for this journey.

Fourth, let us turn to the words "One with each other, / and one in ministry to all the world."[22] They acknowledge that the effects of the Eucharist expand past the limitations of a personal growth experience. The Lord's Supper is a means of grace that leads us into koinonia, a real and deep fellowship with one another. It is a friendship and companionship that is not just for the purposes of enjoyment but for the express intent of carrying us into ministry. As Saliers put it, "Human energies and passions are transformed in light of the passion of God for the world."[23] This is in keeping with the great prayer of Jesus in John 17. Christ's prayer is for not just his disciples but for all subsequent generations of his followers; he prayed not only that God would "protect them in your name that you have given me, so that they may be one, as we are one" but also that "as you have sent me into the world, so I have sent them into the world." He prayed that "they may become completely one, so that the world may know that you have sent me and have loved them even as you have loved me."[24]

Fifth, we turn to the words "Until Christ comes in final victory / and we feast at his heavenly banquet."[25] As we have discussed, Wesley saw the Lord's Supper as a "pledge of heaven," as a foretaste of the glorious feast we will participate in more fully one day.[26]

20. Golitzin, "A Testimony to Christianity as Transfiguration," in Kimbrough, *Orthodox and Wesleyan Spirituality*, 133.
21. The United Methodist Church, *Book of Worship*, 38.
22. The United Methodist Church, *Book of Worship*, 38.
23. Saliers, *Worship as Theology*, 36.
24. John 17:11, 18, 23b.
25. The United Methodist Church, *Book of Worship*, 38.
26. Wesley and Wesley, *Lord's Supper*, 81.

Saliers calls this eschatological theme in eucharistic theology a "radical openness toward the future."[27] These words ensure that the prayer for the Holy Spirit in the United Methodist liturgy is prayed in a way that not only brings the past into our present experience but always ushers in the future. As Stevick has stated:

> Wesley's deepest expectation for the future (and the one most connected with eucharistic experience) may well be that a believer looks forward to reunion with Christ, who waits for his people's coming as they wait for his. One sees Jesus face to face, without the mediation of sacraments, and lives with him . . . Believers anticipate eating and drinking with Jesus in his kingdom, recalling Christ's image and being united with him.[28]

A Spirituality of Becoming

In short, the words of the prayer for the Holy Spirit in the United Methodist Communion liturgy succinctly express the entire flow of thought in this book. The liturgy covers the themes of Christ's presence in the gathering, our remembrance of his sacrifice, our personal sanctification, our spiritual formation as a community, and our tasting of the kingdom of God. Communion is the "grand channel" of grace by which we encounter the risen Christ in our midst, and these are the effects. This is a spirituality of *becoming*. As Brevint put it in his preface, "It enters me into that Mystical Body for which he died."[29] In coming to the table, we are always *becoming* the body of Christ, redeemed by his blood. Again, we pray, "Make them *be* . . . that we might *be*." We encounter Christ's presence, and we are changed. We are sanctified and unified with Christ, and we are grown in unity with one another and in ministry in all the world, in light of the great feast of heaven that awaits us. Something happens here.

---

27. Saliers, *Worship as Theology*, 51.
28. Stevick, *Altar's Fire*, 147.
29. Daniel Brevint, preface to Wesley and Wesley, *Lord's Supper*, 15.

Becoming the Body

I would like to explore how this idea that the presence of Christ in the assembly nourishes us to continually become the body of Christ, redeemed by his blood, reflects an ancient spirituality. In Augustine's fifth-century sermon "On the Nature of the Sacrament," preached on Easter morning to catechumens who had been baptized the night before, he prepares them for their first Communion with vivid imagery:

> If you, therefore, are Christ's body and members, it is your own mystery that is placed on the Lord's table! It is your own mystery that you are receiving! You are saying "Amen" to what you are: your response is a personal signature, affirming your faith. When you hear "The body of Christ," you reply "Amen." Be a member of Christ's body, then, so that your "Amen" may ring true! ...
>
> Remember: bread doesn't come from a single grain, but from many. When you received exorcism, you were "ground." When you were baptized, you were "leavened." When you received the fire of the Holy Spirit, you were "baked." Be what you see; receive what you are ...
>
> Remember, friends, how wine is made. Individual grapes hang together in a bunch, but the juice from them all is mingled to become a single brew. This is the image chosen by Christ our Lord to show how, at his table, the mystery of our unity and peace is solemnly consecrated.[30]

Augustine's fifth-century sermon echoes an even older prayer, found in the *Didache*, that most scholars date to the first century: "As this broken bread was scattered upon the mountains, but was brought together and became one, so let thy Church be gathered together from the ends of the earth into thy Kingdom."[31] Of course, even more ancient than the words of the *Didache* are the words in Scripture itself: "Because there is one bread, we who are many are one body, for we all partake of the one bread."[32] The old saying "You are what you eat" rings strangely true. As the bread has become one, we also become one. No Communion service

---

30. Rotelle, *Works of Saint Augustine*, 7:301.
31. Lake, *Didache*, 19.
32. 1 Cor 10:17.

passes us by without drawing us into participating in its greater purpose as the "grand channel" of grace, opening our hearts for God to change us into what we truly are, whether grace is at work knowingly or unknowingly. Another Augustine Communion sermon emphasizes our becoming:

> And therefore receive and eat the body of Christ, yes, you that have become members of Christ in the body of Christ; receive and drink the blood of Christ. In order not to be scattered and separated, eat what binds you together; in order not to seem cheap in your own estimation, drink the price that was paid for you. Just as this turns into you when you eat and drink it, so you for your part turn into the body of Christ when you live devout and obedient lives.[33]

It is true that we are the body of Christ, but at the same time it is not yet true. We are always becoming what we receive. Life in Christ takes shape in community, and of course community is made up of individuals who are "diamonds in the rough." That's why life in the church never goes perfectly. But what we "get" out of Holy Communion is the continual and radical redefinition of who we are. As Saliers puts it, "Liturgy thus enacts that which devotional prayer alone cannot. The assembly of believers, the gathered body, comes out of the pathos of living and struggling, seeking God together with restless hearts."[34] This is a spirituality of *becoming* expressed in the prayer for the Holy Spirit in our United Methodist liturgy.

When Jesus reclined with the original twelve disciples around the table of an upper room, he gathered them in the context of a Passover meal celebrating their freedom into a new existence. For generations, our Jewish ancestors had done so to get in touch with the liberation of the Exodus. Near the beginning of Brevint's preface in the Wesley brothers' book of eucharistic hymns, he

---

33. Rotelle, *Works of Saint Augustine*, 6:262.

34. Saliers, *Worship as Theology*, 26. For Saliers, "pathos" is the suffering of the world, held in tension with "ethos," the self-giving of God. This is discussed on pp. 22–25.

Becoming the Body

discusses how the symbols become fresh and how this freedom has become alive in Christ:

> Therefore, as at the Passover, the late Jews could say *This is the Lamb, there are the Herbs our Fathers did eat in Egypt;* because these latter Feasts did so effectually represent the former: so at our Holy Communion, which sets before our eyes Christ *our Passover who is sacrificed for us;* our Savior . . . *doubted not to say, This is my Body, when he gave the Disciples the Figure of his Body*: Especially because this Sacrament duly receiv'd, makes the thing which it represents, as really present for our Use, as if it were newly done.[35]

For the Jews, it is remembering the *narrative* that carries power. For Christ, the very embodiment of divine presence, freedom became not only a story to be told but a narrative to be *lived* in the flesh. And in living the story of our freedom from the bondage of sin, the Communion he instituted continues to *become* something that nourishes *us* to become something. In Christ, the meal became about *becoming*.

"Who Thy Mystic Body Are"[36]

The people who come to the table are still broken. We're not always going to be welcoming, sometimes we're going to be downright mean, and social issues will threaten to unravel us. That's not because there is something wrong with the *church*. That's because there is something wrong with *humanity*. The church is the one place where we come together to be who we are already are, knowing that we are "not there yet." We are the body of Christ, and yet we are still becoming. Slowly, we are called into abandoning the cultural myth of the "us and them." There are many images in the Scriptures for what the table is all about, but the most fundamental

---

35. Daniel Brevint, preface to Wesley and Wesley, *Lord's Supper*, 5; italics in the original partially quoted earlier.

36. Charles Wesley, "Christ, from Whom All Blessings Flow," in The United Methodist Church, *United Methodist Hymnal*, no. 550.

is that we are "one body" in Christ. We know full and well we are not one body yet, nevertheless we trust in God, who says we are. It is true but not yet true.

Our reflection on the epiclesis in United Methodist tradition not only resonates with the distinctive bands of color in Wesleyan Communion theology but also reclaims an ancient spirituality. Saint Ignatius of Antioch said in his letter to the Romans, concerning the facing of his own martyrdom, "I am the wheat of God, and let me be ground by the teeth of the wild beasts, that I may be found the pure bread of Christ."[37] There is nothing magical about this transformation of becoming bread for the world; again, a better word for it is "mystical." The church as the body of Christ is neither simply symbol nor merely metaphor; it is a mystical reality.

Over a long period of time, the church lives into this reality. There may be strong resistance within us and among us, but it's reality still, not fantasy. The table is sweeping us into it. We are simply in the season between the "is" and the "ought to be," not at the end of salvation history but at a unique place within the broader movement of God. Charles Wesley put it this way in one of his most well-known hymns, one that is not specifically about Communion or found in the eucharistic collection:

> Christ, from whom all blessings flow,
> perfecting the saints below,
> hear us, who thy nature share,
> who thy mystic body are.[38]

As members of Christ's "mystic body," we are sharing in his nature and being perfected in his love. In summary, in this book, we have explored together the ways in which, for Wesley, the powerful effects of encountering Christ's presence in our Communion gatherings are multifaceted. We experience anew the saving sacrifice of Christ in our present-day offering, we are personally drawn into union with God and perfected in love as the sacrament

37. Schaff, *Apostolic Fathers*, 290.
38. Charles Wesley, "Christ, from Whom All Blessings Flow," in The United Methodist Church, *United Methodist Hymnal*, no. 550.

Becoming the Body

nourishes us through life's struggles, and we feast with one another in light of the great banquet of the kingdom of God, which is being ushered into our very lives. These qualities led Wesley to claim the Eucharist as the "grand channel" of the various means of grace. It's a channel by which we, as sinful and broken people, are nevertheless living into the reality that we are the body of Christ, redeemed by his blood.

This is what is truly distinctive about Wesleyan Communion spirituality, and a fresh rediscovery of this spirituality would have incredible implications for these difficult times in Methodism. As I write, a group of activists within the United Methodist Church has announced the date of the organization of a new breakaway denomination and is now in the process of withdrawing and establishing itself. There have been many times in religious history, including Methodist religious history, where separation has been necessary, I suppose, to move forward in peace. But I can't help but wonder how much our human propensity toward division must grieve the heart of God.

The church of God in history has been like a great river that diverges into many branches. You could look at the various streams of a river and say, "How sad that the river has split in so many places!" Or you could celebrate the reality that because of this tendency of nature, more people have access to the water. I pray that in today's tricky times in North American religious life, we refrain from letting culture wars continue to spill over into the worldwide United Methodist Church. We sometimes try very hard to control and direct (or redirect) the water's flow, but we must remember that we are drinking from what is fundamentally one body of living water. Jesus said, "Come to me, all you that are weary and are carrying heavy burdens, and I will give you rest."[39] The context of his discussion of what to tell John the Baptist makes it clear that for Jesus, all means *all*. Jesus said this to his questioners while he was dealing with their religious prejudice against gentiles. Of course, the Pharisees immediately started picking on him for

---

39. Matt 11:28.

letting his disciples pluck grain on the Sabbath and healing a man with a withered hand (Matt 12:1–14).

We aren't perfect, but we are called to come to the table as God's people ready to build bridges rather than erect walls. There is a meme floating around social media that reads, "I'd rather attend church with messed up people who love God, than religious people who dislike messed up people."[40] I suppose if Judas was invited to the table, everybody is invited to the table. Do we believe that Christ's presence pours out grace upon grace that helps us experience anew the self-giving love of Christ, deepens our love for God and others, and forges a new sense of community in light of the coming kingdom of God, or do we not?

---

40. Capaci, "I'd rather attend church."

8

Reconnecting

WHEN I RECEIVED MY first appointment as a United Methodist student pastor, I was entering my third year of seminary. I was sent to a lovely little church in rural north Alabama. One of the things I was most excited about was finally being able to serve as celebrant for Holy Communion. I simply couldn't wait for the local church's traditional "first Sunday," so we shared Communion on my very first day in the pulpit.

I vividly remember a kind young woman who spoke to me just after the service: "You know what I love the most about Communion? It's just me and Jesus." I loved her sentiment of personal experience with Christ . . . but something didn't feel right. I can now say that I have spent the rest of my life and ministry answering the question that was presented to me on day one. Communion is so very personal, yes. But it's not just about "me and Jesus." It's about Christian community and the kingdom of God. Isn't that the biggest problem with North American Christianity, that we think it's all about "me and Jesus"? As I said earlier, we tend to believe in what I call the "new trinity" (me, myself, and I). But Wesley reminds us we are God's "mystic body," not a bunch of individual Christians.

Something Happens Here

When I ponder the balance of the personal and the communal effects of sharing the sacrament, I think about my first visit to the chapel at the Upper Room, the spirituality center of the United Methodist Church located in Nashville, Tennessee. The chapel is built around a beautiful carving of Leonardo da Vinci's *The Last Supper*, and the room itself is designed with details from the artwork. Upon entry, one immediately feels drawn to the table. When I knelt at the table, I looked up. Because of the mastery of the carver, it appeared as if Christ were looking at me personally. I then realized that no matter your place at the table, Christ was looking you in the eye. The Communion table is the longest table in the world because it stretches across time, space, and culture, yet each of us encounter Christ wherever we are.

Today's culture is fond of driving wedges between people. Do we continue to let this trend spill over into the church and divorce our personal holiness from our call to social holiness? It's one thing to seek the heart of God and search the living Word for guidance over the decisions of life in light of tradition, reason, and experience. It's another thing to attempt to institute this theological task for everyone else. Countless Christians throughout history have practiced discernment and arrived at different conclusions. But instead of inviting people to look to Christ, we tend to ask them to choose sides. This is not discernment in the spirit of the Jerusalem Council in Acts 15. Instead, it quickly becomes intolerance in the spirit of the Pharisees. The Holy Spirit doesn't always choose sides. Sometimes, she shows us a third way, a path beyond our binary ways of thinking.

In the previous chapter, we took a good look at our United Methodist liturgy for Holy Communion in light of all that was truly unique about Wesley's Communion spirituality. We homed in on the words "Make them be for us the body and blood of Christ, / that we may be for the world the body of Christ, / redeemed by his blood," which enliven this distinctiveness.[1] How can we *be* the body of Christ when it is so apparent that the body is broken? Bruce Morrill says that the Eucharist is the "fundamental means

---

1. The United Methodist Church, *Book of Worship*, 38.

Reconnecting

whereby the church shares its common life in the Spirit of Christ and comes to know itself as the body through whom Christ now explicitly lives and acts for the salvation of the world."[2] If so, there is no more pressing need for those who follow the Wesleyan path than to get in touch with our core Communion spirituality during these tumultuous times in the institutional church. There is no other way to come to "know ourselves" as we find our way forward.

The ultimate purpose of this book is to draw conclusions from our study of Wesleyan *distinctiveness* that can make a difference during these times of great *divisiveness* in United Methodism. I would like to frame the remaining discussion of our desperate need to reconnect with our essential Communion spirituality using the wisdom of *The Rebirthing of God: Christianity's Struggle for New Beginnings* by John Philip Newell.[3] I will then invite the reader to hear the stories of two contemporary writers, John Pavlovitz and Sara Miles, who have found themselves coming back to the table as a matter of "practical theology" for these problematic times. Finally, I will propose some ways that reconnecting with essential Wesleyan Communion spirituality will help us navigate this difficult period in faith history.

John Phillip Newell and the Dream of a Reborn Christianity

John Phillip Newell has a dream for the rebirthing of Christianity in these times when institutions are crumbling. He quotes Pierre Teilhard de Chardin, who observed that Christianity is "reaching the end of one of the natural cycles of its existence."[4] Newell chooses not to flee in the face of the death of institutional Christianity as we know it. Instead, he calls for a "radical reorientation of our vision" which is "from deep within the collective soul of

---

2. Morrill, *Encountering Christ*, 17.

3. Newell, *Rebirthing of God*. It is beyond the scope of this book to outline factors that have brought the United Methodist Church to an impasse over differences in biblical interpretation and ethics regarding human sexuality.

4. Pierre Teilhard de Chardin, qtd. in Newell, *Rebirthing of God*, 9.

Christianity."[5] The concept of his book is that we can reconnect with that which is already deep within us as the source of our rebirthing. He invites the reader into "listening for the beat of the Sacred within ourselves and within the body of the earth."[6]

Newell writes of an uncomfortable truth. He says that "much of what is happening within the four walls of our household—liturgically, theologically, spiritually—is irrelevant to the great journey of the earth today and of humanity's most pressing struggles."[7] I suggest that the internal turmoil of institutional churches in North America, which The United Methodist Church is a part of, is distracting us and putting us out of touch with the real struggles and hopes of the world. Newell calls us, first of all, to reconnect with the *earth*, saying, "Humanity has emerged from within the matter of the cosmos. We express the nature of the universe. What is deepest in us—our longing for relationship—reveals a yearning that is within all things."[8] Christ calls us to come back to this longing:

> He is the memory of what we have forgotten—that everything moves in relationship. He comes to lead us not into a detachment from the earth or a separation from the other species and peoples of the world, but into a dance that will bring us back into relationship with all things. He is pointing to what is deepest in the body of the earth and to what is deepest within each of us—the desire to move in harmony.[9]

Second, Newell compels us to reconnect with *compassion*, which is, simply put, "remembering those who suffer."[10] He describes compassionate living as not only a matter of seeing but of "being moved in our guts" like Jesus. In Luke 7, when Jesus saw a woman who had lost her son, he is described as having "compassion for her" (Luke 7:13). The Greek word in the text means being moved

   5. Newell, *Rebirthing of God*, xi.
   6. Newell, *Rebirthing of God*, xvii.
   7. Newell, *Rebirthing of God*, xii.
   8. Newell, *Rebirthing of God*, 6.
   9. Newell, *Rebirthing of God*, 7.
   10. Newell, *Rebirthing of God*, 17.

Reconnecting

with "bowels of compassion."[11] I believe that in the midst of denominational strife, the desire to be right has overwhelmed our desire to be in relationship with each other, and we desperately need to return to this visceral place of being moved from within. Christianity has never been about being *right* over being in *relationship*. It is fundamentally about love of God and love of neighbor. This is something Jesus said clearly and something Wesley certainly confirmed.

Third, Newell invites us to reconnect with the *light*. As he does throughout the book, he makes reference to Iona, a small island off the coast of Scotland. He sees Iona's sacred sites of pilgrimage as "sacraments or living icons through which we glimpse the Light that is everywhere." He experiences it as a "place in which our seeing is renewed, so that when we return to the demanding and conflicted places of our lives and our world we do so with open eyes that have been refreshed."[12] Newell believes this light is within all people, and that it is "deeper than any division."[13] He says that "to shine, we need to keep returning to the places—whether our magnificent religious sanctuaries of Light or earth's natural temples of Light—to remember that we and all things have come into the world to be filled with this Light and to shine."[14] I believe that this imagery of light applies to our struggle, for in times that are most *divisive*, we need to return to what is most *distinctive* about our life at the table so that our "seeing" is renewed and the light of love might shine in the midst of upheaval.

Fourth, Newell encourages us to reconnect with the *journey*. He makes a case that Christianity has gotten to a place in our history where we do not need to think of ourselves as competing with the other religions of the world but being in relationship with them. He quotes a Canadian Mohawk elder who wonders what the Western world would be like "if the mission that had come to us from Europe centuries ago had come expecting to find light in us."[15] He

---

11. Newell, *Rebirthing of God*, 22.
12. Newell, *Rebirthing of God*, 32.
13. Newell, *Rebirthing of God*, 34.
14. Newell, *Rebirthing of God*, 39.
15. Newell, *Rebirthing of God*, 47.

critiques the tendency in the Western church to "absolutize" our religion. He says, "Instead of viewing it as a road sign that points beyond itself, we consider it a stop sign. It becomes the destination, the end. When that happens, it becomes confused with the Ultimate Reality that is always beyond utterance, beyond embodiment, beyond form."[16] I believe that in the journey of North American religion, the level of entrenchment on both traditionalist and progressive sides of the institutional divide over a small number of concerns has become a dead end we cannot seem to move beyond. A fresh look at our life at the table might be just what it takes to enlighten the situation and move us beyond ourselves.

Fifth, Newell calls us to reconnect with *spiritual practice*. This is incredibly relevant to us as we explore our heritage of Wesleyan Communion spirituality! He notes that there is a deep desire to "recover practices from the past to promote the rebirth of spiritual well-being today."[17] He reflects on Thomas Merton's invitation to a contemplative orientation in life. Merton said, "We are living in a world that is absolutely transparent and God is shining through it all the time . . . in people and in things and in nature and in events."[18] But Newell says the problem is that "we don't see it." He adds a phrase that speaks to what we have discussed about what anamnesis, or remembrance, truly is: "Spiritual practice is about remembering to see." He says that for Merton, "spiritual practice is not about an idea or concept of God. It is about seeking the experience of presence."[19]

This presence within is "like pure diamond, blazing with the invisible light of heaven."[20] Newell describes how seeing the diamond essence in everyone and everything is "plunging deep into the heart of the world" in order to "be strong for the work of transformation in the world."[21] I propose that there is no more powerful

16. Newell, *Rebirthing of God*, 51.
17. Newell, *Rebirthing of God*, 59.
18. Thomas Merton, qtd. in Newell, *Rebirthing of God*, 61–62.
19. Newell, *Rebirthing of God*, 61–62.
20. Thomas Merton, qtd. in Newell, *Rebirthing of God*, 65.
21. Newell, *Rebirthing of God*, 68–69, 71.

Reconnecting

way to taste and see the presence of the living God in ourselves and in the world around us than coming back to the table in a fresh way. Wesley would simply love what Newell has to say both about the experience of divine presence and seeing the light of heaven. We must see differently in order to move forward together.

In chapters 6 and 7, Newell calls us to reconnect with *nonviolence* and with the *unconscious*. He discusses Christ's way of nonviolence in terms of Christ's great offering of not just salvation *from* the world but salvation *of* the world.[22] He notes that we may preach nonviolence and yet still be consumed by "violence of heart."[23] The rebirthing of our true depths will involve getting back in touch not only with Christ's call for nonviolence but also with our collective unconscious. He reflects on Carl Jung, proposing that "the way to access these depths is through the world of dreams, intuition, and imagination" with a "river of images, or archetypes . . . which flow deep from within the human soul."[24] I would like to suggest that as the religious landscape of North America is shifting dramatically, the rebirthing of our true depths must involve fresh experience with the love of Christ, and there is no more important way to do this than with the *sacred imagination* of life at the table. Carl Jung himself does so, in fact, when he writes that we need to "celebrate a Last Supper" with our ego.[25] The table is precisely where our unconscious needs to be renewed, in the sacred world of dreaming and imagining what it means to be in communion with one another. For Wesley, this is the "pledge of heaven" effect of our feasting together in all our diversity of life and complexity of thought.[26] We need this divine imagination like we have never needed it before.

Finally, Newell calls us to reconnect with *love*. Reflecting further on Jung, he affirms that the mystery of love is unexplainable and that the briefest description of love in the Scriptures, "God is

---

22. Newell, *Rebirthing of God*, 78.
23. Newell, *Rebirthing of God*, 84.
24. Newell, *Rebirthing of God*, 91–92.
25. Carl Jung, qtd. in Newell, *Rebirthing of God*, 99.
26. Wesley, *Lord's Supper*, 81.

love" (1 John 4:8), is probably also the most profound. Reflecting on the cross, he finds that "the only force that has the power to truly bring together the apparent opposites in our lives and our world is love."[27] He reflects on Simone Weil, who "believed that the cross was a revelation of our capacity for love"—not our ego's capacity but our soul's capacity. Newell comments, "This is not the strength of the small self. It is the strength of the Great Self at the very heart of our being."[28] Weil said, "The real presence of God is the beauty of the universe."[29] For Newell, this presence is certainly not confined to one particular religious tradition or sacramental action. But I believe that this chapter brings our discussion full circle to the imperative we have in The United Methodist Church: we must get back to a sense of the presence of Christ in the Communion gathering. For the church, there is no other way to love beyond our human ability to love than returning to the "grand channel" of grace.

If you have read this far, you may have surmised that Newell's concept of *reconnecting* with that which is deepest within us is very close to a Wesleyan understanding of anamnesis. What is deepest in us is our identity as children of God and as members of the body of Christ. This is Merton's "pure diamond." As Holy Communion brings the sacred story of the sacrificial love of Christ into fresh and present experience, we reconnect in the greatest of imaginative ways with compassion, with a love that shines like the sun, and with the presence of the living Christ. As we gather for a foretaste of divine glory, we reconnect with our deepest longing for relationship, with a new way of seeing, and with a sense of the holy that moves us beyond ourselves.

This reconnecting, this remembrance, is the greatest hope we have for these divisive times. To reframe the words of Wesley, Newell, and Morrill, Holy Communion is the grand channel of grace with which we must get in touch to reconnect with who we are at the deepest level and whereby we come to know ourselves

---

27. Newell, *Rebirthing of God*, 105–6.
28. Newell, *Rebirthing of God*, 116.
29. Simone Weil, qtd. in Newell, *Rebirthing of God*, 113.

Reconnecting

again. As a United Methodist, I recall that fresh reconnection with the table has been a *centerpiece* of a number of renewal movements in American Methodism before, from eighteenth-century circuit riding, to the turn-of-the-century licensing of local pastors under the supervision of traveling elders, to the era of nineteenth-century camp meetings, to early twentieth-century revivalism, to the more recent renewal movements of the Walk to Emmaus and the Academy for Spiritual Formation. The Eucharist has been before, and will be again, what reconnects us with who we truly are. It is part of what energizes a refreshing wave of the Holy Spirit. Of course, it would be overly simplistic to make reconnecting with the practice of Communion the sole source of our hope during trying times. But for American Methodism, the question becomes one of how this time of rebirthing, when the church as we know it is being reinvented, is both *expressed* by life at the table and *formed* by life at the table.

We have used the wisdom of John Phillip Newell to paint a picture of where The United Methodist Church finds itself in its struggle for new beginnings, as well as how imperative it is to reconnect with the distinctive nature of Wesleyan eucharistic spirituality. Now we will turn to two fresh expressions of what it means to reconnect with the table during divisive times. John Pavlovitz and Sara Miles might be considered writers in the broad general category of "progressive evangelicals." Each of them speaks with an important voice among those finding their way back to the Communion table in this time of crisis in American religion. At the same time, their voices stand in helpful contrast, since Pavlovitz speaks from the perspective of the conceptual and Miles writes from the perspective of the practical.

John Pavlovitz and the Vision of a Bigger Table

John Pavlovitz's book *A Bigger Table: Building Messy, Authentic, and Hopeful Spiritual Community* embarks on a vision of Communion spirituality. The image of the "bigger table," the prevailing concept of the book, is the prism through which he sees the issues of present-day culture regarding exclusion and inclusion. Pavlovitz begins with his experience of studying for ministry while working a college job in a café among a community of gay men. He notes, "The heart is a rather curious entity. Once its doors swing wide open, they can't easily be shut again."[30] His ministry began in the midst of a small community where all kinds of people "had a standing invitation, not to receive charity from someone morally superior and not to serve as religious projects to be converted and fixed—but as welcome dinner guests of a hospitable Jesus who modeled what happens when we break bread with the broken."[31]

Along the way, he discovered that his brother was gay: "This is the gift that relationship gives you . . . When you are faced with the reality of having an LGBTQ family member or close friend, it forces you to hold up your theology to see what it's really made of. And when this happens, some of it gets confirmed, some of it gets shifted, and some of it blows up."[32] Pavlovitz reconnected with the church when he got married, attending a Methodist church with a hospitable female pastor. He notes that "despite their claims of gracious hospitality, churches are often far more aggressive than they'd like to admit."[33]

This experiential starting place led him to a lengthy commentary on the state of the church and the need for a "bigger table." He believes the culture wars that have dominated churches the last fifty years have been "a reliable way to generate urgency among the faithful and to get people worked up." He reminds us that if reality is framed in terms of warring sides, "you'll eventually see the Church and those around you in the same way too. You'll begin to filter the world through the lens of conflict. Everything becomes a threat to the family; everyone becomes a potential enemy." Religion becomes cold and cruel, "pushing from the table people who aren't part of the brotherhood and don't march in lockstep with

---

30. Pavlovitz, *Bigger Table*, 13.
31. Pavlovitz, *Bigger Table*, 14.
32. Pavlovitz, *Bigger Table*, 17.
33. Pavlovitz, *Bigger Table*, 27.

Reconnecting

the others."[34] He notes that sadly, differences which could expand the table of our understanding have become divisive and polarizing instead. He comments, "Clearly defined, rigid systems are far easier to establish and maintain than the muddy, far more ambiguous process of sharing life together."[35]

Pavlovitz made what he considers his most fundamental choice in ministry—to err on the side of love: "When you simply accept those around you in whatever condition they come to you, the table naturally expands."[36] The Communion table became the eye through which Pavlovitz sees the ministry of the church in the world. He says, "The table was an altar around which [Jesus] welcomed the world to experience communion with God and one another. We easily forget that faith is a relational experience, that it is almost impossible to move into Christlikeness without other souls to extend compassion and mercy and love to, or to receive those things from."[37] For him, life at the table is not just about liturgy but about how to be in ministry with each other. He discusses the diverse people Jesus did meal ministry with, noting that "for him the table is a tool of connection. It transcends difference. It bridges disagreement. It declares the other welcomed and worthy of hearing. It recognizes the other and declares commonality with him or her. I don't see very much of this in the modern Christian expression here in America."[38]

In short, the "bigger table" is Pavlovitz's way of describing Communion as a foretaste of glory divine, a vision that propels us as we move forward in history. He notes:

> This is what it means to be the people of the bigger table: to look for the threads that might tie us together and to believe that these are more powerful than we imagine. This is the only future the church really has. Disparate people will not be brought together through a denomination or

---

34. Pavlovitz, *Bigger Table*, 28.
35. Pavlovitz, *Bigger Table*, 45.
36. Pavlovitz, *Bigger Table*, 43.
37. Pavlovitz, *Bigger Table*, 58.
38. Pavlovitz, *Bigger Table*, 58–60.

a pastor or by anything the institutional church can offer. We know that now. These were useful for a time, but they are an exercise in diminishing returns.[39]

Pavlovitz describes this table as a table with four legs: "radical hospitality," "total authenticity," "true diversity," and "agenda-free community."[40] He summarizes, "This is the very heart of the bigger table. It isn't about formulating and defending some ironclad religious system that we proof-text and memorize and attempt to convince others to adopt. It's not about winning theological discussions or defending world views. It is about tangibly living in a way that responds to what we believe about our own belovedness and about the belovedness of those we live alongside."[41]

The voice of John Pavlovitz is an important one. We are witnessing a massive, slow-moving breakdown of the religious institutions we have grown to love, which seem to be falling apart at the seams of ordination and marriage, though I would argue the issues that divide us run much deeper. In the midst of this, his voice is a voice of *reimagining*. But this reimagining is not a matter of abandoning what is most sacred about the church; it is a matter of *reconnecting* with it. Our life at the table is not just a personal exchange of confession for forgiveness, or a monthly recharge of our spiritual batteries, or an object lesson to remind us mentally that Jesus died for our sins. We must not let our Communion practice in North America continue to be influenced by what Don Saliers calls "the privatization of ethical concerns."[42] Communion is an encounter with the living Christ that changes the way we live and love in the world. It is less about remembering with our *brains* and more about remembrance with our *bones*. It is a foretaste that propels us to live for the vision of the kingdom. Like Pavlovitz, we must come to proclaim, "I am holding out hope for true communion."[43]

39. Pavlovitz, *Bigger Table*, 62.
40. See Pavlovitz, *Bigger Table*, 65–102.
41. Pavlovitz, *Bigger Table*, 118.
42. Saliers, *Worship as Theology*, 171.
43. Pavlovitz, *Bigger Table*, 172.

Reconnecting

Sara Miles and Becoming Bread for the World

Sara Miles is less conceptual and much earthier and more practical than Pavlovitz in her experience of coming back to the table to move forward through these tumultuous times. Her very first time receiving Holy Communion, she experienced herself becoming part of the body of Christ, redeemed by his blood. In *Take This Bread: The Spiritual Memoir of a Twenty-First-Century Christian*, she tells of one morning at age forty-six when she walked into a church, ate a piece of bread, and took a sip of wine, which was "a routine Sunday activity for tens of millions of Americans—except that up until that moment I'd led a thoroughly secular life, at best indifferent to religion, more often appalled by its fundamentalist crusades. This was my first communion. It changed everything." This led her—a self-described left-wing journalist, skeptic, and lesbian—to a faith that she had always scorned. She writes, "Mine is a personal story of an unexpected and terribly inconvenient Christian conversion."[44]

Her years of serving food in the restaurant industry, followed by seeing the church at work with the poor in Nicaragua, was grace that had prepared her for this new awakening. She says, "As with everything else I'd learned—as with the religion I would come to practice—I absorbed cooking through my body." She adds, "I had no idea then that what I was hungry for was communion."[45] Miles asks, "So why did communion move me? Why did I feel as if I were being entered and taken over, completely stirred up by someone whose name I'd only spoken before as a casual expletive? I couldn't reconcile the experience with anything I knew or had been told. But neither could I go away: For some inexplicable reason, I wanted that bread again . . . when I opened my mouth and swallowed, everything changed. It was real."[46]

This was her entry point into really grappling with the Gospel. Over time, she discovered that the kingdom of God Jesus lived and

---

44. Miles, *Take This Bread*, xi–xii.
45. Miles, *Take This Bread*, 32–34.
46. Miles, *Take This Bread*, 60–61.

died for was a place where the proud were scattered and the powerful rebuked, where the hungry were filled with good things and the rich sent away empty. This kept bringing her back to the table:

> The entire contradictory package of Christianity was present in the Eucharist. A sign of unconditional acceptance and forgiveness, it was doled out and rationed to insiders; a sign of unity, it divided people; a sign of the most common and ordinary human reality, it was rarefied and theorized nearly to death. And yet that meal remained, through all the centuries, more powerful than any attempts to manage it. It reconciled, if only for a minute, all of God's creation, revealing that, without exception, we were members of one body, God's body, in endless diversity. The feast showed us how to re-member what had been dis-membered by human attempts to separate and divide, judge and cast out, select or punish. At the table, sharing food, we were brought into the ongoing work of making creation whole.[47]

This realization caused Miles to engage the Gospel in a way that changed the very direction of her life: "As I interpreted it, Jesus invited notorious wrongdoers to his table, airily discarded all the religious rules of the day, and fed whoever showed up, by the thousands. In the end, he was murdered for eating with the wrong people. And then—here's where the story got irrational . . . I believed this God rose from the dead to have breakfast with his friends." The story of Jesus saying, "Feed my sheep" (John 21:17), became her calling.[48]

Much of the rest of the book is testimony about Miles developing a city-wide community food bank ministry, starting at her own local church in San Francisco: "And there was that vision of a Table where everyone was welcome. Our neighbors, friends and strangers, were hungry. The very least a Christian church could do, for starters, was feed them."[49] She launched this city-wide food

---

47. Miles, *Take This Bread*, 76–77.
48. Miles, *Take This Bread*, 92.
49. Miles, *Take This Bread*, 108.

Reconnecting

ministry the very same week that she was baptized. She says, "I understood why Christians imagined the kingdom of heaven as a feast: a banquet where nobody was excluded, where the weakest and most broken, the worst sinners and outcasts, were honored guests who welcomed one another in peace and shared their food."[50] The pantry ministry grew and grew. Miles writes, "The pantry looked like the kingdom to me precisely because we were all thrown in together—a makeshift community so much bigger and more contradictory than any of us would have chosen."[51]

The voice of Sara Miles is also an important one for these strange and difficult times. Unlike Pavlovitz, her experience was hardly theoretical. She became in a vivid and practical way a participant in the body of Christ, broken and given for the life of the world. She became the bread that fed. Hers is not a voice of reimagining but a voice of *becoming*. She lived and breathed the prayer "Make them be for us the body and blood of Christ, / that we may be for the world the body of Christ, / redeemed by his blood."[52]

Pavlovitz and Miles can teach us that both reimaging and becoming are the principal ways of reconnecting with life at the table. Pavlovitz witnesses to the visionary dimensions of life at the table, and Miles witnesses to the power of the Lord's Supper to sanctify us and move us toward perfection in love. Wesley would be so pleased that their encounters with the presence of Christ at the table compelled them to experience anew his sacrificial love and that this encounter with Jesus led them to places of reimagining and becoming in these difficult times. Miles muses, "I didn't realize right away what I was doing, because Jesus' meal had left the building."[53]

---

50. Miles, *Take This Bread*, 158.
51. Miles, *Take This Bread*, 222.
52. The United Methodist Church, *Book of Worship*, 38.
53. Miles, *Take This Bread*, 269.

Something Happens Here

Coming Back to the Table in Order to Move Forward

Painting a picture with Newell, Pavlovitz, and Miles gives us a vivid sense of what the church must do to reconnect with what is deepest within us in these times of institutional crisis in North American religion. As Beatrice Bruteau has put it, "In the evolution of our consciousness, we may be said to be standing on the threshold of an era having a renewed sense of unity, of wholeness, of relations that draw together, of insight that grasps in a single vision, of universal inclusiveness."[54] This is a matter of reconnecting with Bruteau's "communion consciousness" discussed in a previous chapter.[55] There is no doubt that the church is changing and we are on the cusp of a new era in North American religious life, even as we ride the waves of culture wars that ripple into the church in a way that threatens to rip us apart. The question is whether we will sell our soul to keep the institutions we hold dear up and running, or if we will be about the sacred task of reclaiming what is most precious and deep in the core of our being, our life as people of the table. Could we, would we, *dare* we come back to the table in order to move forward into the future?

Geoffrey Wainwright laments that most Communion theology of the past in academia has focused exclusively on the question of presence in the elements, the eucharistic sacrifice, and the benefits to those who receive it instead of the "ecclesiological consequences" of experiencing the meal as anticipation of the great banquet. He says there are "consequences for the church's *mission* as a messenger of the kingdom, and for the church's *unity* as the body of Christ."[56] For Wainwright, this is the spiritual power of the fact that Communion is a *meal*.[57] This was important for Wesley, for whom the Lord's Supper was never a private experience with Jesus. It is a means of grace in all its fullness precisely because the presence of Christ was experienced in a *shared* meal. It is a presence

---

54. Bruteau, *Grand Option*, 49.
55. Bruteau, *Grand Option*, 50.
56. Wainwright, *Eucharist and Eschatology*, 2–3, 7.
57. Wainwright, *Eucharist and Eschatology*, 21.

Reconnecting

which enlivens the sacrificial love of Christ, perfects us as people of love, and draws us into unity in light of the great feast of love.

During these difficult times, those who follow the Wesleyan path must have a fresh encounter with what is truly distinctive about our spirituality of the Lord's Supper. Most importantly, this involves faithfulness to the practice itself, trusting God to use it as a means of grace no matter what our future holds. But it also involves doing at least three things to reconnect with what is deepest within us.

First, we must let Communion be the prism through which we see clearly both where we truly are and where we ought to be. As I discussed at length in the first chapter, it seems to me that the apostle Paul did exactly that. He addressed the large-scale divisiveness embedded in the community life of the church of Corinth by taking a careful look at their table practices and going from there. Table manners were not really the problem here. What he saw happening at the table illuminated the truth of the deeper division, disrespect, and lack of regard they had for each other. Like in Paul's day, I say a fresh experience with our distinctive sacramental spirituality would lift Communion up to become the lens through which we see the colors of what is beneath the surface of our institutional brokenness. We can then build a theology that will move us forward, just as Paul did with chapter 12 on the body of Christ with many parts, chapter 13 on the "more excellent way" of love (1 Cor 12:31), chapter 14 with all its practical advice on spiritual arrogance, and chapter 15 that keeps an eye on heaven... *all* of which flow from his observations at the table. Paul is both honest about what he saw at the table in Corinth and forthright in articulating a robust theology that emerged from that experience. This came from his deep yearning for those he loved, that they might live into what it means to be people of love within a community of love.

The meat of this book has been discovering the sense in which Wesley did all this as well for his time and in his context. I suggest we need to do so all over again. United Methodists must navigate our present conflict through the looking glass of "Communion consciousness" and thereby trust the table to be the "grand channel" of grace. What do we see when we look through the lens? It is clear we are divided, and if we look closely at the colors of our live and love together, the divisiveness is not just about human sexuality. It is about many things, such as power, money, and regional influence. We know this because once groups on the edges of Methodism have openly stated that they are planning to leave the denomination, these dynamics came to the surface. I am convinced that none of this conflict originated within the church or from our faithful interpretation of Scripture. It is clearly from culture wars that have spilled over into the church.

There is a "more excellent way," and it is the way of love, just as it was for the Corinthians. Paul never said that love would be easy, but he did describe it with vivid and beautiful language that came from his "Communion consciousness." There is an emerging voice that is asking how we can stay at the table together after all, not simply tolerating our differences while trying to institute one position or the other but embracing our differences in a whole new vision of what it means to be the church. Yes, we must accept amicable separation by those on either edge who no longer want to be part of the main body, but for the denomination itself, there will be new life at the table. After all, it's not our table; it's Christ's table, and *all* of us are there by his gracious invitation. Like Paul, we need to begin to write prolifically about this more excellent way and what it will look like. I hope we can begin to use the kind of poetic and powerful language that he did.

Second, we must let the Lord's Table dramatically change our underlying assumptions. We must be willing to embrace what we find when we begin to see with this new "Communion consciousness." This is the spirituality of *reimagining* that Pavlovitz embodies, letting this consciousness usher the kingdom of God into our midst. In modern North American culture, we like to be *right* and we like to be *rich*. Perhaps this is the reason that fundamentalism and prosperity are two uniquely American derivatives of true Christianity, as noted earlier. Communion is not an event to fit into our busy schedule to stay on God's good side or to "get something out of it" like a good American consumer. We don't *do*

Reconnecting

worship; we *join* it. Communion is entry into a life. Its power is not limited to the emotions of the moment but is expanded by a rhythm of a lifetime of "constant" Communion.

Holy Communion, in time, may change what we expect from it, including the assumption that we know everything we need to know. The story of the road to Emmaus in Luke 24 narrates the way the presence of Christ changes these perceptions. The disciples did not recognize him when they were walking on the road. Once he broke bread and his presence was revealed, they said, "Were not our hearts burning within us while he was talking with us on the road, while he was opening the scriptures to us?" (Luke 24:32). He had just disappeared before their very eyes, but this impressive stunt is not what they were enamored with. They did not say, "Wasn't that a fantastic trick?" Instead, they said, "Weren't our hearts burning?" It dawned on them how much he had changed their perceptions by his very presence, hidden as it may have been, on the road. At that table on the way to Emmaus, the presence of Christ was not located in the bread and cup. It was both on the road and in the room, but this perception-altering presence was now made known in the breaking of bread.

In North American churches, our underlying assumption has been that there is an unresolvable conflict, and most of us think our side is right, whichever "side" that might be. Those who are prone to take a side do not seem to see any other way but one way to approach these ecclesiastical matters. But what if our underlying assumption were that there are millions of people in the mix that simply want to love and to serve in their local context, and more and more are beginning to believe that allowing space for others to interpret Scripture through tradition, reason, and experience differently than us does not threaten our identity? Christ would call us to embrace the muddiness of staying together at the table with those who do not understand us and even those who sin against us. After all, that is exactly what Jesus did on the night he was betrayed, and that's what he told us Christian love truly is. May God give us the grace to see that something new is being born and that Christ has been walking with us in this holy struggle in ways that are still hidden from our eyes. May we hear him speak the truth of where we are right now and who we could become together as the body of Christ, and may his Word resound in our hearts like burning fire.

Third, we must let Communion re-form our identity. The spirituality of *becoming* that Miles embodies so well is the ultimate witness to the power of the Lord's Supper for our spiritual formation. We are called to *be* the body of Christ, redeemed by his blood. We are always becoming that which we eat and drink. As broken and sinful as we are, this is the mystery of our true identity, so it is less important to be *right* than it is to be in *relationship* with God and one another. What we "get" out of Communion is a continual and radical new definition of who we are.

Wesleyans are deeply committed to a life of both personal and social holiness. An overemphasis on personal morality, as if the only issue that matters is what constitutes right and wrong behavior, has in North American religious culture overshadowed a balanced emphasis on corporate ethics. Questions of exclusion and inclusion are *by far* the more central issues of the Gospels themselves. Yes, there are difficult details to work out as a church, and splintering may be the likely scenario for now in history. But we come to the table with hope. We trust that in Communion is "the present *image* of what will be made *manifest*."[58] The very definition of community in the body of Christ is that we are in this together, with others that are different than us and that we might not agree with, and we are nevertheless being crafted into one by the grace of God. As Wainwright says, "To put the matter in one sentence: the eucharist has an inescapable missionary significance in so far as it is the sign of the great feast which God will offer in the final kingdom to express forever the universal triumph of his saving will and purpose."[59]

When Jesus gathered his disciples together for the Last Supper in each of the Synoptic Gospels, they were scared and confused. Jesus had warned them about his death, but they really had no idea how their mission was going to play out in light of the

---

58. Wainwright, *Eucharist and Eschatology*, 66.
59. Wainwright, *Eucharist and Eschatology*, 159.

terrible things that were about to happen. So, he sat with them, and he ate with them, and he celebrated the Passover with them in a way that blew their minds. One might ask why the church should focus on Communion when there is so much struggle and division going on in the church in North America. The answer is simple. We do it for the *same reasons Jesus did*.

This chapter on reconnecting with the table must, of course, conclude with the words of the Wesley brothers. One particular eucharistic hymn includes multiple threads of the distinctive teachings we have discussed. It gives us a unique call to encounter, in Christ's "virtuous" presence beyond the elements themselves, a wondrous grace that fills us with *all* the life of God. "Sure and real" is this grace that "meets" us and "perfects us in One." It is my fervent prayer that grace does meet us in this difficult moment, for Communion may be our best hope. May this be our song:

> O The Depth of Love Divine,
>   Th' Unfathomable Grace!
> Who shall say how Bread and Wine
>   GOD into Man conveys?
> *How* the Bread his Flesh imparts,
>   *How* the Wine transmits his Blood,
> Fills his Faithful Peoples Hearts
>   With all the Life of GOD!
>
> Let the wisest Mortal shew
>   How we the Grace receive:
> Feeble Elements bestow
>   A Power not theirs to give:
> Who explains the Wondrous Way?
>   How thro' these the Virtue came?
> These the Virtue did convey,
>   Yet still remain the same.
>
> How can heavenly Spirits rise
>   By earthly Matter fed,
> Drink herewith Divine Supplys
>   And eat immortal Bread?
> Ask the Father's Wisdom *how*;
>   Him that did the Means ordain

Something Happens Here

Angels round our Altars bow
    To search it out, in vain.

Sure and real is the Grace,
    The Manner be unknown;
Only meet us in thy Ways
    And perfect us in One,
Let us taste the heavenly Powers,
    LORD, we ask for Nothing more;
Thine to bless, 'Tis only Ours
    To wonder, and adore.[60]

---

60. Wesley and Wesley, *Lord's Supper*, 41.

Postlude

ONE OF THE MOST potent experiences of my pastoral journey began when Madalyn "lit into me" after church one day. It was an otherwise typical Sunday morning at the beginning of Advent, and I had no idea when I was receiving the brunt of her anger that she was going to teach me something quite wonderful about Communion. I was destined to behold a significant transformation in her because of life at the table.

Madalyn was a dear friend in the church I was serving. Her children were active in youth group, and she served faithfully in various forms of leadership. She was serious about Bible study and would press me with thoughtful questions. Occasionally, she dropped by my study to talk about theology or to bring me a gift of her artistry. She was pleasant to be with, and I loved her dearly.

On that first Sunday of Advent, not long after her husband was stationed overseas, she got rather upset. During worship, we had pondered one of the scriptural names in Old Testament prophesy for the long-awaited Messiah. I had asked what our lives would be like in a world prone to war and violence if we *really* believed Jesus was our Prince of Peace.

Well, she *really* let me have it after the service! In front of a dozen stunned parishioners, she exclaimed, "You have no idea how much what you said hurts families of people who are deployed overseas!" I was taken aback and quickly searched my memory to recall what I might have said that lacked honor for those who serve

Postlude

our country, for that was certainly not my intent. I did my best to listen. I gently reminded her I had acknowledged in the sermon that we have a tradition in the church of "just war theory" which sees that sometimes war is necessary and must be waged with appropriate boundaries, though the Word consistently reminds us that war is never truly God's plan for humanity. My endeavor to calm her spirit was to no avail.

In the evening, we had a fellowship dinner at the church. She came to me again, this time speaking slowly and apologetically: "I'm so sorry I blasted you this morning. All afternoon, I have been going over what you said in your sermon, and I guess you didn't really say anything wrong. I suppose all preachers are against war." We talked for a while, and she was openhearted and thoughtful. "To be honest, I think I just really miss my husband." My heart went out to her.

The following Sunday morning, we gathered for Holy Communion. I noticed the earnest look on her face as she knelt. The next day, Madalyn dropped by my office in her usual way. "All week, I've been feeling very lonely. When I went forward for Communion yesterday, I realized it's one of many times I'm going to have to come to the table without my husband. But then I started thinking about how fortunate I am. So many people don't even have their husband anymore. I don't really understand it, but I feel like God is calling me to do something." I promised to keep the conversation open and hold her in prayer.

The following week, she dropped by again. "Do we take Communion to people who are shut-ins?" Something had nudged her. Over the next few weeks, Madalyn became the organizer and leader of what we called Diakonos,[1] a ministry to extend the Communion table by delivering the blessed bread and cup from our table to the homebound each month with a cordial visit from a trained layperson.

---

1. *Diakonos* is New Testament Greek for "deacon." In Acts 6:1–7, seven deacons were chosen to oversee the distribution of food, giving apostles the ability to focus on the ministry of the word.

Postlude

I learned so much from walking with Madalyn through her amazing journey. The intersection of life and the Gospel had created a crisis for her, as it most certainly can. In the honest sharing of Christian community, she felt safe in saying what was on her mind. As a result of being heard, she got in touch with the empty places in her own life. As she came back to the Communion table, she was drawn beyond her brokenness to a place of deep compassion.

In time, she had become what she most longed for herself, a source of comfort and presence in times of great loneliness. I have never seen such a clear and traceable deepening of "sacramental permeability"[2] in someone's life over the course of just a few weeks. She *worshiped* on that Sunday morning in Advent all right, but these things shifted in her not just because of one worship experience, or even because of a series of them. It happened because of her lifetime journey of coming to the table, which had shaped and formed her in Christian love. When life got tough, the table itself was a focal point for her transformation.

Three Great Obstacles

What will it take for us to be overwhelmingly changed by this table we love so dearly because of its love poured out so freely? I believe that for many of us in the United States, this will involve moving past certain obstacles by the grace of God, as well as embracing the call of Newell to reconnect with our deepest roots at the table.

In modern life, there are at least three great obstructions to overcome if we are to open our hearts to the life-changing nature of the sacraments. The first is that we are culturally "wired" to be *consumers*. As I have implied earlier, when we let our consumerism spill over into our worship expectations, we come to church to "get something out of it." We desire a new principle we can apply to make our lives more successful. We want a shot of inspiration so we can go change the world. We are impressed with great music

---

2. "Sacramental permeability" is discussed in Bieler and Schottroff, *Eucharist*. The term refers to the way in which the Eucharist is meant to penetrate, or pass through, every part of life.

Postlude

or a talented preacher because quality worship has been well produced, and a fine production is something a consumer craves.

When we do not have a highly emotional experience or gain a radically new perspective because of attending a service, there is a part of us that is disappointed. We think there is something wrong with the local church, with the pastor, with the church in general, or with us. The problem is not that we long for inspiration. The problem is that we think of worship as an event rather than a life. Experiencing the permeability of the sacraments is a long-term adventure.

The greatest gift of Communion is not limited to the moment we receive it. Communion is not a wrapped present that can be opened all at once. Worship is a rhythm, a life that unfolds. The Eucharist progressively shapes us over time. It gives us transformational space to encounter that which is beyond our senses. Sometimes, its impact is hardly noticeable. But encountering the holy presence of Christ pervades us "from one degree of glory to another."[3] The Lord's Supper always blesses us, whether it feels fantastic or mundane on a given Sunday. It forms us in mysterious, even undetectable ways. At best, we may be able to look back over a long time, even a lifetime, and see its effects. Like marriage, which sees its fullest joy walking through a lifetime of laughter and tears, the effects of worship are not limited to a singular experience. It is a rhythm we are invited to, and rhythm is how the transformation happens.

Communion is not a funeral for Jesus but rather a celebration of his resurrection that transforms us into people of the resurrection. The mystery of the Eucharist is that we are not consumers just taking it all in. We are continually becoming the body of Christ, redeemed by his blood. We must trust in the "slow work of God."[4]

If consumerism is one of the great obstacles to fully experiencing the transformative gift of Communion over time, a second great cultural obstacle is *functionalism*. This is our tendency to evaluate everything based on its production value. If we give an honest look at Americanized Christianity, we see that we make

3. 2 Cor 3:18.
4. Harter, *Hearts on Fire*, 102.

Postlude

worship about many "practical" things. We infuse it with politics or prosperity, making it about being right or getting rich. We use the Bible to make a point, supporting our preconceived notions and often pointing at others while we are at it. We feel we should be getting something out of Jesus when we do something for Jesus. When we boil it down to the difference it makes, we mimic our assumptions from the culture of the marketplace[5] and come to the table to get the forgiveness we need this month. Trading is exactly what the table does *not* do. It is a window into the kingdom of God, an invitation into greater mystery.

Years ago, Sandy and I lived in a parsonage that happened to be on the invisible migration trail for a massive flock of birds. Every year, thousands of them came through. I would enjoy catching a glimpse of them and pausing to sit for a while and behold the beauty of their majestic movement. Once, I happened to be driving home from a meeting in another town when I discovered the contour of the highway ran parallel to this migration trail. For over two miles, I drove with a seemingly infinite number of birds that were flying like one large, flowing black ribbon through the sky. It was a mystical experience, as if I were lifted into another reality, an alternative movement of the Spirit I had become a part of.

This is what coming to the table is about. Again, we don't *do* worship. We *join* it. We become part of what God is doing over a vast number of generations and cultures to draw the world back to Godself.[6] Our very gathering around the table is a small window into a larger gathering of the ages. This is the very definition of who we are as the church, the *ecclesia*.[7]

We come to the table not to *do* something in order to *get* something from God. We come because we yearn to continually become part of what God is doing in the world. This radical shift in perspective takes a long time, or a lifetime, of coming to the table

---

5. Bieler and Schottroff, *Eucharist*, 92–102 contrasts the culture of market exchange with the mutual gifting of the sacraments.

6. See John 12:32.

7. *Ecclesia*, or "assembly," as the definition of the church in the New Testament, is discussed at length in Lathrop, *Holy People*.

Postlude

to embrace. We discover the deepest truth about Christian faith, which is that it is not about us. It's about God. The kingdom of God is an ocean we can learn to float in, when all along we thought it was about swimming harder. When we have transformational experiences, like my friend Madalyn, we have been brought to a new place of going with the flow.

If consumerism and functionalism are two great cultural obstacles to overcome in our quest to reconnect with the table, a third is our *cultural concept of freedom*. No word is dearer to the heart of a patriot than "freedom," of course, and this is imbedded in the very DNA of the cultural identity of the United States. This seems to connect with the idea in Scripture, for Paul said to the Galatians, "For freedom Christ has set us free. Stand firm, therefore, and do not submit again to a yoke of slavery."[8] The problem is that we tend to interpret this spiritual freedom through the lens of cultural notions of independence. It is easy to forget that Paul was referring to the freedom from Old Testament law, not freedom from any kind of responsibility for one another. Later in the same chapter, he added, "Only do not use your freedom as an opportunity for self-indulgence, but through love become slaves to one another. For the whole law is summed up in a single commandment, 'You shall love your neighbor as yourself.'"[9] Freedom is a wonderful thing, but from a biblical perspective, it's not so much about independence as it is about *interdependence*.

I recall the infamous 1963 inauguration speech in support of segregation made by Governor George Wallace, mentioned in the Communion story of John Rutland in the prelude of this book. Wallace set forth the idea insidious to white nationalism that the "free heritage" of the people he represents constitutes freedom from the "tyranny that clanks its chains upon the South."[10] Freedom is interpreted as having no responsibility for others, and of course this is a twisting around of the freedoms we enjoy. Can we imagine what it would be like if the people of Corinth complained against

8. Gal 5:1.
9. Gal 5:13b–14.
10. Wallace, *Inaugural Address*, 5.

Postlude

Paul for taking away their freedom? After all, should we not be able to bring whatever food we want to the church meal? No, Paul lets the Communion table teach us that true freedom is the freedom to love and to serve. Along with the obstacles of consumerism and functionalism, this mutated concept of freedom can get in the way of reconnecting with the power and effect of the Communion table as we move forward into the future.

Tasting and Seeing

The psalms compel us to "taste and see that the Lord is good."[11] It is often difficult for us as humans to see past what is, yet at the same time, it is our imagination that defines us. This is true of the human condition, and it is most true as we gather around the Communion table. If we are to reconnect with that which is deepest within us, one way to speak of the table is the psalmist's language of both tasting and seeing. Sara Miles, discussed in the previous chapter, is a prime example of tasting, experiencing what it means to become bread for the world through the practice of Holy Communion. John Pavlovitz, then, is a prime example of seeing, having let Communion become the lens through which he interprets life in the body of Christ. In both cases, their imagination took them to a new place of grace.

Our Celtic Christian siblings often speak of "thin places,"[12] places where the divine and human seem to touch. I have grown to believe that the Communion table is the thinnest place of all, for in the mystery of God's love, these simple acts of eating, drinking, speaking, and gesturing give us a taste of something deeper that it takes a lifetime to see. Our senses, in time, take us beyond our senses into the mystery of God's revelation.

What are we tasting and seeing as we reclaim the distinctiveness of Wesleyan Communion spirituality in these times of divisiveness? At this pivotal moment in the history of The United

---

11. Ps 34:8a.

12. This is a Celtic Christian term for "locales where the distance between heaven and earth collapses" (Weiner, "Heaven and Earth," 1).

Postlude

Methodist Church, we are being changed, whether we like it or not. The crisis due to the raging culture wars in the United States has imposed itself on the church, yes. But the question of where we go from here is a sacramental question, not a purely institutional one.

John Wesley's entire exercise of plumbing the depths of *his* tradition to reclaim the distinctiveness of what he called "primitive" Christianity was *his* sacramental answer to *his* institutional dilemma early in ministry in Georgia. Then, a few decades later, after his mission work in America was concluded, culture had evolved to a pivotal point in North American religious history. As the father of the Methodist movement, he was forced from afar to deal with the obstacles that sentiments around the American Revolution would bring. So, founding the distinct ministry orders of stationed local pastor and traveling elder in the newly established Methodist Episcopal Church balanced his evangelical fervor for spreading scriptural holiness throughout the frontier with reconnecting with that which was deepest in himself and in his tradition. He continued to reclaim the Communion spirit of the English Nonjurors. He maintained his embrace of the teaching on personal sanctification of the Eastern fathers and mothers. He carried on with his fascination with the heartfelt piety of the Moravian movement.

His ministry had appeared on the scene in a very controversial and difficult time in English religious life, and he chose to go back to the table in order to move forward in ministry. Then, in the end, he was not satisfied with the idea of evangelizing America with what Anglicanism had *become*. He gave new language and a new structure to that which was already deep within them which threated to be lost. That was the brilliance of our original Methodism. We must do the same.

We, too, have the opportunity to search the depths of our own tradition for the enduring and precious gems that will carry us forward in history. If we are to thrive again, it is because we will reclaim this creative combination of progressive Evangelicalism and historic sacramentalism. "Evangelicalism" in the United States has become something other than what is deeply imbedded in our own identity. In some quarters, rather than drawing people into a

Postlude

radically transforming relationship with Christ and trusting God for the rest, it has become fused with politics and has tapped into the underbelly of divisive cultural issues. The United Methodist Church is on the verge of having minority groups splinter away not because of doctrinal issues rooted in either the Gospels or creeds but because of the culture wars of recent decades. We need to reach farther back to rectify this. We have reached a pivotal moment when we must plumb our own depths again and rediscover who we really are. In times of great institutional anxiety, Communion focuses us on what's truly in front of us. We are people of the table.

Over time, coming back to the table will take us to another place—a place of dwelling in the larger picture, of flying with the great flock, of what some theologians call "eschatological imagination."[13] Coming back to the table takes us from our cultural tendency to radically redefine the Gospel to a place of allowing the Gospel to radically redefine our contemporary experience. This is what makes worship, and the sacraments in particular, unique art forms. They tie the past, present, and future together into a grand movement of grace. Just as the table brings ancient Scripture to life in present experience, it is at the same time a foretaste of glory divine. As we feast in this in-between place, we set the table not for ourselves, and not simply for each other—we are setting the table for the whole world to come.

Life does not revolve around me, and it doesn't revolve around my denomination. It doesn't revolve around North American culture, and it doesn't revolve around a certain political ideology. It revolves around the table, which patterns our lives in light of God's new creation. The table is dynamic, and it is relational. It strikes us, messes with us, and niggles with us. It "comforts the afflicted" and "afflicts the comfortable."[14] It creates holy space, transformational space for the Spirit to work. Like my friend Madalyn, we bring all of who we are to all of who God is. And by tasting, we begin to see.

---

13. Saliers, *Worship as Theology*, 49–68.

14. This phrase is commonly used regarding various subjects, such as worship, social action, and journalism. It is attributed to Finley Peter Dunne, American humorist and writer (see Hoag, "Preachers Echoing Finley").

Postlude

Becoming Love Poured Out

I have a Communion chalice that I keep on my shelf. It's my favorite sacramental cup, aside from special ones given to me as gifts. I found it at a local pottery shop in North Carolina and was completely captivated by it. I thought this earthy, blue vessel was the most beautiful one I had ever seen.

It occurred to me one day that the purpose of this chalice is not to sit pretty on my shelf. It was made for so much more, yet I leave it on display most of the time. I suppose we are like that. We are created in the image of our gracious and loving God for more than we can possibly imagine, yet sometimes we find ourselves sitting pretty in church, as if that is what's important.

Reflecting with my chalice in hand that day, I began to think that the real purpose of this cup is not to sit there; it is to be filled. We come to a place in the Christian life when we discover that we are called beyond the ministry of showing up. This longing is evident in our prayer and praise as we sing, "Fill my cup, Lord, I lift it up, Lord."[15] We yearn to be filled by the Holy Spirit, to be completely saturated with the love of God.

Yet, upon further reflection on the pottery vessel in my hand, I realized that this is not the ultimate purpose of the chalice either. As I tipped my wonderful blue cup over on its side in my hands, I began to see that the purpose of it is not to be filled. The ultimate purpose of this chalice is to be emptied. It is to be poured out.

This is our spirituality of becoming what we share at the table. Eucharist is the intentional, redemptive, self-emptying love of God poured out. There have been many teachings throughout history on the atonement, the work of God for our redemption. These have taken shape in different ways over the centuries. Perhaps the most prominent theories are the ransom theory and the substitution theory.[16] I am at a place in my journey where I am a fan of

---

15. Richard Blanchard, "Fill My Cup, Lord," in The United Methodist Church, *United Methodist Hymnal*, no. 641.

16. There are multiple theories of the atonement which are beyond the scope of this book. No compelling theory prevails in Christendom.

Postlude

neither. The ideas of ransom and substitution are indeed rooted in Scripture as the early church began to unpack the meaning of the cross. But I believe these are best seen as metaphors and illustrations that fall short of giving us a comprehensive theory on how we are reconciled with God. In the end, placing all our eggs in one of their baskets just doesn't make sense.

What does our liturgy and eucharistic practice reveal to us about redemption? What better place to look than the first Christian hymn we have record of. Scholars agree that Paul is reciting the words to an ancient Christian hymn. It sings:

> Let the same mind be in you that was in Christ Jesus,
> > who, though he was in the form of God,
> > > did not regard equality with God
> > > as something to be exploited,
> > but emptied himself,
> > > taking the form of a slave,
> > > being born in human likeness.
> And being found in human form,
> > he humbled himself
> > > and became obedient to the point of death—
> > > even death on a cross.[17]

The table is the ultimate, redemptive expression of God's intentional, self-emptying love. There is no good news in a god who doesn't get involved. God feels the brokenness of our division, and the wounded heart of Jesus is healing us in the broken places. Christ is the great reconciler in divisive times. It turns out that the overturned chalice in my hand a few years ago gave me a pretty good understanding of Christian life, because that is what Jesus did for us. He poured himself out. That is the meaning of what love is, and life is not about being filled up but about being emptied out for others.

The secret to experiencing great joy in Communion is knowing that we never quite figure it out. The table is not about some "flat" sense of inclusion, because its grace is rooted in the brokenness of bread. But we don't come because we have all the answers;

---

17. Phil 2:5–11.

Postlude

and the more we come, the deeper the questions get. It is about mystery unfolding and grace abounding. Its truth takes a lifetime to embrace, and it is bigger than the present moment. Like a holiday meal with family, it not only nourishes us for the moment but carries with it traditions, relationships, memories, and identity. There is power beyond a singular experience. A lifetime of coming leads to *becoming*.

I have made the claim that something happens at the table. What has Wesley showed us about this? Real presence is experienced here. Fresh renewal takes place here. Depth of love emerges in us over time, and authentic community is shaped by our glimpse of heaven. The experience of Holy Communion is both intensely personal and significantly corporate. Grace pours out here, and transformation happens here. The kingdom of God may take us to places we have not yet imagined, but thankfully, Christianity has never been limited by human imagination. Communion is just that—a meal of divine imagination. It is my hope that coming back to the table as the "grand channel" of grace might help the church become all we were created to be for the future.

May we reconnect with the mystery of Christ's presence for such a time as this. May we rekindle the holy fire that burns within each of us. May we be willing to be shaped and formed into a new community in light of heaven. May we be the body of Christ, redeemed by his blood.

About the Author

STEVE WEST DESCRIBES HIMSELF as a husband, father, minister, musician, and writer. His wife and best friend, Sandy, is a retired clergywoman, and they have two grown children. Steve and Sandy live in Jacksonville, Alabama, where he serves as senior pastor of First United Methodist Church. He enjoys writing and blogging, singing, playing piano and trombone, camping, hiking, mountain biking, coin collecting, and genealogy.

Steve has been a pastor for over thirty years in the North Alabama Conference and has been a delegate to the Jurisdictional Conference, chair of the annual conference Worship Planning Team, chair of the Order of Elders, and long-term member of the Board of Ordained Ministry. He presently serves on his bishop's Context Team, representing centrist voices in conversation with others over what it will look like to move forward as The United Methodist Church in our context. He was highly instrumental in launching the Stay UMC movement in North Alabama. In 2020, he gained national attention with an open letter, "Why I Am Not Leaving the United Methodist Church," which went viral and was published in various places. His doctoral studies on Wesleyan Communion spirituality impacted his views on our present impasse. He continues to be active in ministries of discipleship and spiritual formation in the annual conference.

Steve has led worship music for SoulFeast at Lake Junaluska and at a variety of other retreats and spiritual formation

About the Author

experiences. He is a child of Sumatanga, a Methodist retreat center in the mountains of northeast Alabama, and has been in leadership in Music and Arts Week and the Alabama Emmaus Community. He is active in the Academy for Spiritual Formation and has served as retreat leader or worship coordinator and musician at numerous Five-Day and Two-Year Academies from Alabama to Wisconsin, Indiana, Florida, and even Singapore. He was the principal musician and producer for the "Songs for Morning Prayer" CD for the twenty-fifth anniversary of the Academy for Spiritual Formation and has served as a faculty presenter for the Academy on the subject of this book.

Steve graduated magna cum laude in 1987 with a bachelor of arts degree from Birmingham-Southern College, studying sociology and music. He graduated cum laude with a master of divinity degree from Candler School of Theology at Emory University in 1991 and with a doctor of ministry degree from the University of the South at Sewanee in 2020. He is a published author of newspaper columns, devotional articles, hymn texts, and musical resources. Some of the most significant works are found in *Alive Now*, including "The Exile of Grief," "The Dance of Praise," "A Meditation on Ruby Falls," and "Racoons Are Welcome." His ordination hymn text, "Lord, You Call Us to Your Service," cowritten with Bishop Will Willimon, was published in the hymnal *Celebrating Grace*. His hymn text "Water and Spirit" was published in *Alive Now*, and he has liturgy published in *Worship and Song: For United Methodists*. His Communion anthem, "This Is the Table of Welcome," was written with Nylea Butler-Moore and published by Abingdon Press. He has been a frequent columnist for *The Huntsville Times* and *The Arab Tribune*. For a complete list of publications, see his blog, "Musings of a Musical Preacher."

Bibliography

Bieler, Andrea, and Luise Schottroff. *The Eucharist: Bodies, Bread and Resurrection*. Minneapolis: Fortress, 2007.
Bonhoeffer, Dietrich. *Life Together: The Classic Exploration of Christian Community*. New York: Harper & Row, 1954.
Bowmer, John C. *The Sacrament of the Lord's Supper in Early Methodism*. Westminster, UK: Dacre, 1951.
Bradshaw, Paul F., and Maxwell E. Johnson. *The Eucharistic Liturgies: Their Evolution and Interpretation*. Collegeville, MN: Liturgical, 1989.
Broxap, Henry. *The Later Non-jurors*. Cambridge: Cambridge University Press, 1924.
Bruteau, Beatrice. *The Grand Option: Personal Transformation and a New Creation*. Notre Dame, IN: University of Notre Dame Press, 2001.
Capaci, Eric (@ericcapaci). "I'd rather attend church with messed up people who love God, than religious people who dislike messed up people." Twitter, August 18, 2019. https://twitter.com/ericcapaci/status/1163047329324253184.
Cornwall, Robert D. "The Theologies of the Nonjurors: A Historiographical Essay." *Cromohs—Cyber Review of Modern Historiography*, July 1, 2006. https://doi.org/10.13128/cromohs-11255.
Eslinger, Richard L. *Preaching and the Holy Mystery: The Eucharist as Context and Resource for Proclamation*. Franklinville, NJ: Order of St. Luke, 2016.
Hammond, Geordan. "High Church Anglican Influences on John Wesley's Conception of Primitive Christianity, 1732–1735." *Anglican and Episcopal History* 78 (June 2009) 174–207. https://www.jstor.org/stable/42612802.
———. "The Wesleys' Sacramental Theology and Practice in Georgia." In *Proceedings of the Charles Wesley Society*, edited by S T Kimbrough, Jr., 53–73. Vol. 13. Nashville: United Methodist Board of Discipleship, 2009.
Harter, Michael, ed. *Hearts on Fire: Praying with Jesuits*. Chicago: Loyola, 2005.
Hefling, Charles. "Scotland: Episcopalians and Nonjurors." In *The Oxford Guide to the Book of Common Prayer*, edited by Charles Hefling and Cynthia Shattuck, 166–75. Oxford: Oxford University Press, 2006.

Bibliography

Hoag, Gary. "Preachers Echoing Finley Peter Dunne: The Gospel Comforts the Afflicted and Afflicts the Comfortable." August 2, 2013. https://generositymonk.com/2013/08/02/preachers-echoing-finley-peter-dunne-the-gospel-comforts-the-afflicted-and-afflicts-the-comfortable/.

Kimbrough, S T, Jr., ed. *Orthodox and Wesleyan Spirituality*. Crestwood, NY: St. Vladimir's Seminary Press, 2002.

Lake, Kirsopp, trans. *The Didache: The Teaching of the Twelve Apostles*. London: William Heinemann, 1912.

Lathrop, Gordon W. *Holy People: A Liturgical Ecclesiology*. Minneapolis: Ausburg Fortress, 1999.

The Methodist Church. *The Methodist Hymnal*. Nashville: Methodist Publishing House, 1966.

Miles, Sara. *Take This Bread: The Spiritual Memoir of a Twenty-First-Century Christian*. New York: Ballantine, 2008.

Morrill, Bruce. *Anamnesis as Dangerous Memory: Political and Liturgical Theology in Dialogue*. Collegeville, MN: Liturgical, 2000.

———. *Encountering Christ in the Eucharist: The Paschal Mystery in People, Word, and Sacrament*. Mahwah, NJ: Paulist, 2012.

Neal, Gregory S. *Grace upon Grace: Sacramental Theology in the Christian Life*. Bloomington, IN: WestBow, 2014.

Newell, John Philip. *The Rebirthing of God: Christianity's Struggle for New Beginnings*. Woodstock, VT: SkyLight Paths, 2014.

Ollard, Sidney L., ed. *The Dictionary of English Church History*. Oxford: Mowbray & Co., 1919. https://openlibrary.org/books/OL13505145M/A_dictionary_of_English_church_history.

Outler, Albert C., and Richard P. Heitzenrater. *John Wesley's Sermons: An Anthology*. Nashville: Abingdon, 1991.

Palladius of Aspuna. *The Lausiac History*. Collegeville, MN: Liturgical, 2015.

Pavlovitz, John. *A Bigger Table: Building Messy, Authentic, and Hopeful Spiritual Community*. Louisville: Westminster John Knox, 2017.

Pseudo-Macarius. *Fifty Spiritual Homilies*. Translated by George A. Malloney. Mahwah, NJ: Paulist, 1992.

Rotelle, John E., ed. *The Works of Saint Augustine: A Translation for the Twenty-First Century*. Vols. 6–7. Hyde Park, NY: New City, 1993.

Saliers, Don E. *Worship as Theology: Foretaste of Glory Divine*. Nashville: Abingdon, 1994.

Schaff, Philip. *The Apostolic Fathers with Justin Martyr and Irenaeus*. Ante-Nicene Fathers 1. Omaha, NE: Patristic, 2019.

Schmemann, Alexander. *For the Life of the World: Sacraments and Orthodoxy*. Crestwood, NJ: St. Vladimir's Seminary Press, 1973.

Schmemann, Alexander, and Paul Kachur. *The Eucharist: Sacrament of the Kingdom*. Crestwood, NJ: St. Vladimir's Seminary Press, 2003.

Snyder, Howard A. "John Wesley and Macarius the Egyptian." *Asbury Theological Journal* 45 (1990) 55–60. https://place.asburyseminary.edu/asburyjournal/vol45/iss2/5.

Bibliography

Stevick, Daniel B. *The Altar's Fire: Charles Wesley's Hymns on the Lord's Supper, 1745 Introduction and Exposition*. London: Epworth, 2004.

Stutzman, Paul Fike. *Recovering the Love Feast: Broadening Our Eucharistic Celebrations*. Eugene, OR: Wipf & Stock, 2011.

The United Methodist Church. *The Book of Worship of the United Methodist Church*. Nashville: United Methodist, 1992.

———. *The United Methodist Book of Discipline*. Nashville: United Methodist, 2016.

———. *The United Methodist Hymnal*. Nashville: United Methodist, 1989.

Wainwright, Geoffrey. *Eucharist and Eschatology*. Franklinville, NJ: Order of Saint Luke, 2002.

Wallace, George. *Inaugural Address of Governor George Wallace, Which Was Delivered at the Capitol in Montgomery, Alabama*. January 14, 1963. Alabama Governor Administrative Files, 1958–68. Alabama Department of Archives and History. https://digital.archives.alabama.gov/digital/collection/voices/id/2952.

Washington, James Melvin, ed. *A Testament of Hope: The Essential Writings of Martin Luther King, Jr.* San Francisco: Harper & Row, 1986.

Weiner, Eric. "Where Heaven and Earth Come Closer." *New York Times*, March 9, 2012. https://www.nytimes.com/2012/03/11/travel/thin-places-where-we-are-jolted-out-of-old-ways-of-seeing-the-world.html.

Wesley, John, and Charles Wesley. *Hymns and Sacred Poems*. 1739. Facsimile of the first edition. Madison, NJ: Charles Wesley Society, 2007.

———. *Hymns on the Lord's Supper with a Preface Concerning the Christian Sacrament and Sacrifice, Extracted from Doctor Brevint*. 1745. Facsimile of the first edition. Madison, NJ: Charles Wesley Society, 1995.

Wesley, John. *Explanatory Notes upon the New Testament*. 1755. Facsimile edition, London: Conference Office, 1813.

———. *Sermons on Several Occasions*. Vol 2. London: J. Kershaw, 1825. https://www.google.com/books/edition/Sermons_on_Several_Occasions/dR7cVoxjOGEC?hl=en&gbpv=0.

Whaling, Frank, ed. *John and Charles Wesley: Selected Prayers, Hymns, Journal Notes, Sermons, Letters and Treatises*. Classics of Western Spirituality. Mahwah, NJ: Paulist, 1981.

www.ingramcontent.com/pod-product-compliance
Lightning Source LLC
Chambersburg PA
CBHW051938160426
43198CB00013B/2204